Me:
Selling Who You Are, What You Do, & Why You Matter to the World

Donald P. Roy, Ph.D.
Colby B. Jubenville, Ph.D.

ISBN-13: 978-1535537780
ISBN-10: 1535537787

DEDICATION

To Sara, for her unwavering support and belief in me.
To Chris, Sidney, and Ethan, for being the embodiment of an authentic personal brand.

—Don Roy

To my meaning (Katie), makeup (MB) and message (Jack). You each have your own personal brand that makes you unique. I love you!

—Colby Jubenville

CONTENTS

ACKNOWLEDGEMENTS

Don Roy

A project of this magnitude is the result of the contributions of many people regardless of whether they know they had an impact.

Some people definitely knew they had an impact. My family put up with my countless hours in front of a computer researching and writing. Also, thanks to my colleagues at Middle Tennessee State University for their unwavering support. Their confidence in me has always been a source of strength. A special thank you to Drew Ruble for his assistance in the latter stages of this project.

Countless other people had an indirect impact over many years, most of whom are people I have never met. Many thought leaders in the marketing, personal branding, and self-help space have touched me through a book, presentation, blog post, or video. The cumulative effect has been life changing, inspiring me to leave a marketing career to pursue a doctoral degree in business over twenty years ago. Their work moves me to strive to become better at what I do.

Colby Jubenville

To "My People"

This book is about personal branding and is dedicated to the many students I have taught along the way. There is no greater moment as an educator than when a student takes the time to send me a note, call or email letting a teacher know about their success and the impact they are having in the communities they live, work and play. As a young boy my mom said to me, "follow your dreams and the money will come." Little did she know that she was "planting seeds" for me to not only prosper financially, but also have graduates return to campus and say, "because of the investment you made in me – my life is better."

My Thanks

First, I would like to thank my mother, Karen, and my dad, Wayne, for their vision of what tomorrow could bring. It's easy to "connect the dots" after IT happens. It's quite another story to "connect the dots" prior to IT happening. IT simply defined is being intentional about the person you want to become and the life you want to live.

Second, I want to thank my wife, Katie, for her continued support for what I do and loving my personal brand, listening when things don't go my way and always looking ahead and not behind. I also thank her for our family Jack (14) and Mary Burke (11). I love watching both of you develop your meaning, make up and message.

Third, I would like to thank Mr. John Floyd, founder and CEO of Ole South Properties and quite a personal brand of his own. He has been a mentor to me and continues to let me know what 10 years ahead looks like for me and how to fight for the life, liberty and happiness we want. Thanks for what you have done for me personally and professionally.

Fourth, I would like to thank Mr. Warren Brent for his approach to building relationships, telling the truth and leaving a legacy. While we are just getting started, I am excited to see where we are headed. Learning concepts like "agreed upon reality" and "agreed upon future" changes the game. So thank you.

Last, thank you to all the coaches and teachers I have had along the way. From St. Paul's School in Mobile, Alabama to Millsaps College in Jackson, Mississippi, where I was awoken to what it meant to become a student of the process, and ultimately to The University of Southern Mississippi. Without question it's my unique perspective, education and experience from each of these institutions that make up my personal brand.

A Word of Recognition

No book could be written without burrowing from others. To the many people that we cite in this book I say "thank you" for taking the time to share your knowledge. Lee Brower once said, "If a life is worth living, it's worth writing down." Hopefully, a piece of this book will be worth it to you.

FOREWORD

Ben Hanback

One of my favorite movies ever, hands down, is Cameron Crowe's "Jerry Maguire." The scene that's always stood out to me the most is the moment when Jerry gets fired. As he leaves the sports agency he'd been with, he grabs the office goldfish and vows:

"...if anybody else wants to come with me, this moment will be the moment of something real and fun and inspiring in this godforsaken business and we will do it together! Who's coming with me?"

In the movie, Jerry is a successful, passionate sports agent who wakes up one day struggling to find purpose in life. He cares for his clients deeply and wants to help them grow. But suddenly he's forced to reinvent *his* own brand with the only client that will follow him.

Jerry *really* could have used this book.

When I started my sales career in 1991, I wanted to make sure I set myself apart from the competition. Like Jerry Maguire, I cared deeply about my clients and customers, and yet I also needed to differentiate myself and build my brand. I had to define who I was and why I mattered. I wanted my clients to think about me in a different way, to build relationships so strong that it would be difficult for them NOT to do business with me. With that same sense of purpose, Don Roy and Colby Jubenville will help YOU find the meaning, make-up and message of your brand, so that you, too, can take your career and relationships to new levels.

Throughout this book, Roy and Jubenville provide the blueprint and execution strategy for building your own personal brand – and it's a fantastic ride! Regardless of age, industry, or experience, they will help you define who you are and why you matter in today's business world.

Don and I connected through both sports and a similar fascination with marketing. His insights and expertise in marketing and brand relationships is invaluable, and he provided me a vital marketing vision when I first launched my own business.

Colby has worked closely with my company in developing a local branding strategy. We share a love of sports and family, as well as a passion for building relationships. He has been instrumental in taking my team and my personal development to the next level.

Ben Hanback has enjoyed a 25-year career in the insurance industry in executive roles with Unum, AON, Regions Insurance Group, and as owner of The Hanback Group. A four-year letterman in track at the University of Memphis, Ben is a contributor to The Tennessean, writing articles on business and leadership. He has a long-time association with the Make-A-Wish Foundation as a supporter and volunteer.

INTRODUCTION

You hold in your hands more than a book; it is an instruction manual for creating your personal brand. We know the love-hate relationship many of us have with instructions. Sometimes, we follow instructions for a while but stray from them when they become too complicated or vague. Other times, we forgo instructions altogether under the belief that we can "figure it out." And, we may be able to figure it out with some success. Ultimately, the choice not to follow instructions can leave us with a less than ideal outcome, like assembling a piece of furniture with a couple of screws left over. We do not know what to do with the screws because we did not follow instructions and hope that the unused screws do not come back to haunt us later.

Your own brand is too valuable to be left to chance or following only those instructions that you find easy or comfortable.

Three Questions behind this Book

You may be reading this book because you want to transform your personal brand. Or, you may be reading this book because someone has made it a requirement- a teacher or boss has given you an assignment to complete. Regardless of where you are coming from as you begin reading this book, reflect on three important questions that inspired us to share our instruction set for personal branding: 1) Why me? 2) Why not me? 3) If not me, then who?

Why Me?

It is possible you were taken aback by the book's title: Me. If you are a millennial (often defined as persons born between 1981 and 1995), you are tired of labels associated with your generational group of "self-centered" and "self-absorbed." A book about "me" seems to play to those labels. Contrary to that notion, a decision to proactively market yourself has positive connotations. First, no one else in this world has the incentive or urgency to manage your brand that you have- not parents, spouse, friends, or boss- only you. These important people in your life can support you as you build and maintain your brand, but they cannot do it for you as

1

well as you can do it for yourself. Second, managing your personal brand creates value for the people with whom you interact or serve. The personal benefit to you in terms of professional growth, income, and satisfaction are by-products of the value you add in others' lives. So, far from being a venture in self-indulgence, personal branding is an ongoing process of creating benefit for the world around you.

Why Not Me?

Personal branding is an ongoing concern just as brand management is an ongoing concern for companies and products. However, do not look at managing your brand as a burden to bear or price to pay. Rather, you will enjoy the fruits of proactively managing your professional and personal identity. You should not be excluded from the potential growth that managing your personal brand offers. As you observe others who have "made it," consider that they most likely earned whatever success or status they have attained- it was not handed to them. Similarly, you can be that person other people notice moving up and ahead because of your commitment to nurture your brand. Give yourself permission to grow through building a distinctive personal brand.

If Not Me, Then Who?

It is not surprising that many people hold themselves back through fear of failure. They cannot fathom what will happen to them or what others will think of them if they do not land their dream job, do not get the promotion, fail at a major project, or lose their job. Some level of fear is natural and can even be motivational, driving you to overcome limiting fears to achieve goals. But, another fear that may be more surprising is fear of success. "How will my relationships change if I am promoted?" or "What will my new goals be if I reach my current ones?" Yes, we can be afraid of what we will encounter if we actually get what we want.

The combination of fear of failure and fear of success can serve to sabotage our growth plans, ensuring we do not get hurt… except that is exactly what happens when we limit our own growth. Could someone else step up? Yes, but do not shortchange yourself. Do not defer to others at the expense of your own growth and advancement. A clearly defined personal brand will give you confidence and direction to deal with and overcome the dual threat of fear of failure and fear of success.

What to Expect

This book is divided into five sections. First, you will become acquainted with our concept of a personal brand in Chapter 1. Specifically, you will be introduced to the three "Ms" of a personal brand- Meaning, Makeup, and Message- as well as learn why personal branding is no longer an optional strategy for managing your professional identity. A great deal of misinformation exists about what personal branding is, and we debunk personal branding myths in Chapter 2. The basics of branding are discussed in Chapter 3 as we recognize some readers will be familiar with branding terminology and practices while others have little or no familiarity with branding.

The next three parts of the book is devoted to one of the three Ms of personal branding. Part Two focuses on establishing brand Meaning. Purpose (Chapter 4), Passion (Chapter 5), Situation Analysis (Chapter 6), and Goal Setting (Chapter 7) are the elements of Meaning that lay a foundation upon which your brand is built. Part Three delves into brand Makeup, the skills, education, experience, and knowledge you have that can be used to create value for others. Discussion of brand Makeup components focuses on skill set (Chapter 8), mind set (Chapter 9), network (Chapter 10), and brand positioning (Chapter 11). Part Four explores the Message dimension of your brand. The role of storytelling (Chapter 12), social media in general and LinkedIn in particular (Chapter 13 and Chapter 14, respectively), creating brand content (Chapter 15), and your résumé (Chapter 16) are communication tools that play a role in expressing your Meaning and Makeup to the world.

The fifth section contains the concluding chapter that describes a fourth M. We are going to save it for Chapter 17. All we can tell you is it is a perfect bow to tie onto your brand, making it complete.

Developing Me

A weakness of many personal development books is that while they may share many ideas, readers are not engaged to put the ideas to work for themselves. You will get maximum benefit from this book by accepting our challenge to apply the three Ms of personal branding to yourself. Two resources are available that put the "personal" in personal branding. First, at the end of each chapter you will find a section titled Take Action. You need to do just that- take action- by applying our instructions for building a personal brand to you and your situation. You can learn what makes a distinctive personal brand by reading the chapters, but only you can implement our ideas to spur brand development.

Second, we have partnered with Harrison Assessments to offer several personal evaluation instruments you can access online. Harrison Assessments, created by psychologist Dr. Dan Harrison, are used by organizations in forty countries to assist in hiring, developing, and promoting employees. The Harrison Assessments team has reviewed the content of *Me* and identified eight assessment packages relevant to our 3Ms model of personal branding. A link to these assessments is included following the Take Action section of the chapters for which they are applicable. Although Harrison Assessment reports are not free, the insight you could gain from completing one or more of these self-assessments could be a valuable investment for gaining a deeper understanding of your own brand.

It's time to embark on the most exciting and important marketing project you will ever undertake!

PART ONE:
THE BASICS

1.

THE PATH TO YOUR DREAM JOB

"Regardless of age, regardless of position, regardless of the business we happen to be in, all of us need to understand the importance of branding. We are CEOs of our own companies: Me Inc. To be in business today, our most important job is to be head marketer for the brand called You."
—Tom Peters

Allow us to introduce you to Joshua and Lauren, two soon-to-be college graduates. Each has persevered steadfastly through their undergraduate programs in marketing and public relations, respectively. In the near future, each will be finished with school and will once and for all shift their focus from studying for exams to launching their professional careers.

Joshua and Lauren will graduate from college on the same day; but their similarities pretty much end there. Joshua feels that he benefited from putting all of his available time into his classes (he works 30 hours a week at a sporting goods store in addition to being a full-time student). In large part because of those commitments, Joshua decided to put off his professional job search until after graduation. His jam-packed school and work schedule was also the reason he did not join any professional organizations or pursue any internships while enrolled at the university. Joshua likes school and finds marketing interesting, but even now on the cusp of graduation he is unsure about exactly what types of jobs he should pursue. Joshua says he is going to stop by and see his favorite professor soon to ask for advice on how to go about finding a job.

Lauren has had a hectic final year, too. She completed an internship in addition of her class schedule and even spent her weekends playing in a band with three friends. However, Lauren has also done something that Joshua has been "too busy" to think about; namely, apply the marketing concepts she learned while in her college classes to boost her professional career preparation. So, for instance, Lauren narrowed her interests to specific job opportunities she sought—event marketing and management. She identified a total of 11 businesses in cities desirable to her where solid entry-level opportunities existed, some with reputable public relations firms and others with solid companies that employ PR professionals. She joined event management groups on LinkedIn and began following companies and professionals in that industry on Twitter.

Lauren also reached out to a fellow alumnus of her college who was a former student of her adviser, met with her to learn more about her job and company, and is now maintaining frequent contact with her. Her internship with a sports marketing agency provided her both insight and hands-on experience into planning corporate hospitality events. Lauren now believes she has discovered a passion for helping clients entertain and impress and is eager for college to end so she can begin her first post-college job with a public relations firm that ranked high on her targeted list of prospective employers.

Do You Know Them?

Chances are you know Joshua and Lauren, or at least people who fit their descriptions. Whether your emphasis is in marketing, public relations, engineering, biology, or any other field, virtually all professions share a characteristic common with product industries: competitors as divergent as Joshua and Lauren vying for the same opportunities and growth.

If you were attracted to reading this book, we feel confident that you too are vying for opportunity and growth. To seize those two desires, though, you must adopt a strategic approach (like Lauren's) that will give you a competitive advantage and produce the greatest chance to succeed against others battling for the same positions and promotions.

What is that strategic approach? It is the concept of personal branding. By applying to your personal brand many of the same concepts that have contributed to market dominance by iconic brands such as Coca-Cola and Gillette and younger brands like Amazon and Zappos, you can develop a distinctive identity that differentiates you from other professionals vying for the same results in your field.

Simply put, you are more than just a worker with credentials like a college degree. From a professional perspective, you are a brand!

So What Brand Are You?

First, congratulations are in order! You have been given an awesome responsibility: brand manager for the world's most important brand…You! (Refer again to the quote that launched this chapter by business management author and speaker Tom Peters.) Your personal brand is the most important brand in the world (at least it is and should be from your perspective), and no one has the power to exert influence over it like you do.

Now, if the idea of managing your career using processes similar to what top marketers have used to manage the brands of mainstay products or services is unsettling to you, relax and take heart—you are not the first person to feel that way. However, instead of feeling overwhelmed or unworthy of such a role, look at it from a positive, long-term perspective instead. Practicing personal branding can be beneficial in helping you not just establish your career plan but also manage your professional identity over the course of your entire professional career. Personal branding is an ongoing process for identifying, developing, and communicating your unique value both to yourself and to others. The goal of personal branding is to purposefully and permanently position yourself as someone possessing meaningful differences that set you apart from the competition. Isn't that what you want? Fear is no obstacle when the potential reward is so dear.

Explaining personal branding using definitions is certainly useful; but perhaps a case in point can better serve to flesh out the benefits of proactively managing your professional identity. Kelley, a 2003 college graduate with a degree in mass communications, has spent the years following her graduation in sales and marketing positions with five different companies. Each time she has moved to a new company, she has assumed a more significant position, effectively advancing her career rather than simply "job hopping."

What is her secret? It's not her degree, or even her years of experience (although those are quite helpful and often necessary for certain opportunities). Her real strength is that her personal brand is incredibly consistent and positive. She has developed a reputation among customers and colleagues alike throughout her field as a salesperson who is very knowledgeable about her industry, pays attention to detail, and who cares about outcomes. Her communications always reinforce her professionalism. Kelley's target market is thereby consistently attracted to her "brand" because it clearly signals the value that she has to offer. This is her "leg up" on the competition. And it's what makes all the difference in her climb up the corporate ladder.

Personal branding is a process for identifying, developing, and communicating your unique value.

Why Personal Branding?

You might still be skeptical about the need to practice personal branding. Before we go any further, then, here are three reasons why you should drop the doubts and embrace the personal title of Manager of the World's Most Important Brand: You!

News Flash: You Have Competition

Unless you go to work in the family business or venture out as an entrepreneur, you will always be marketing yourself to be hired by someone. As if that isn't enough of an uphill battle, you will also have plenty of other people around you doing the very same thing and trying to get the very same job.

According to the National Center for Education Statistics, more than 1.8 million undergraduate degrees and 750,000 graduate degrees were awarded by colleges and universities in the United States in 2012-2013.[1] Now, mind you, that is only the number of newly minted graduates entering the professional workforce. A whole additional layer of competition is also in play when you factor in those people who are already in your industry of choice looking for a new or better position (not to mention graduates from previous years who are still looking to land a job in their chosen field of study).

Underemployment, a situation in which people whose qualifications (education or experience) exceed the requirements of the job they hold, has grown exponentially among college graduates in recent years. It is estimated that 284,000 college graduates are currently working in minimum wage jobs. That figure is double what it was prior to the economic recession of 2008.[2] What explains that perplexing, almost unthinkable situation? Layoffs triggered by the recession put many experienced professionals out of work. Their re-entry into the workforce gave employers the choice of more experienced talent from which to choose and put recent graduates at a distinct competitive disadvantage. The underemployment rate for recent college graduates is now about 40%.[3]

Are you ready to face this environment? Are you already in it and fighting to stay ahead or even in place? Believe me when we say that as a professional, you will have competition even if you are your own boss. Consultants, freelancers, and other contract-based workers are another significant strata of professional (read: competition) increasingly grabbing their piece of the professional pie, and they too must position themselves to compete against others (like you) with similar expertise.

Here's a "for instance." If you have aspirations of working as a social media professional, you are certainly not alone in our modern, technology-driven world. A review of Twitter profiles to identify social media professionals yielded more than 180,000 mentions either as "experts," "evangelists," "gurus," "consultants," or other, similar positioning descriptors.[4] That's a lot of people! And a lot of smart people, too! So what is your answer for sticking out in a pack of 180,000 other professionals?

Personal branding can empower you to craft a distinctive identity that can help elevate you above the "noise" of thousands of other self-proclaimed "ninjas" and "masters" in your profession, transforming you in to the true go-to expert or professional you want people to perceive you to be.

News Flash #2: You Need to Stand Out

Once you have a firmer grasp on the extent of the competition you will face to land a job in your field or with a particular company, it should become quite evident to you how easy it is to become lost in a sea of applicants and résumés.

For example, sports marketing is a field that attracts many college students, as well as people in the workforce looking to make a career change. The appeal of the industry—working in entertainment around people and events that the general public is highly interested in—means that any open position in the field attracts many applicants. It is not uncommon for a professional sports team to receive hundreds of applications for a single entry-level ticket sales job or low-paying (or often unpaid) marketing internship.

Regardless of the number of applicants vying for the same position as you, though, it is likely that at some point in the winnowing down of qualified candidates the competition will become intense. Whether you are up against three or 103 fellow "competitors" for a job, your challenge is clearly to stand out from the pack.

Let's be clear before going any further that standing out does not necessarily mean tangibly standing out. Yes, you could wear a bright orange blazer as your "signature look," or you could print your résumé using a purple-colored font...; but that is not the standard definition of standing out. You may have heard the saying "you can put lipstick on a pig, but it's still a pig." That holds true with resumes and job applicants as well. Bypass these base approaches and aim instead to develop a distinctive difference valued by employers. Personal branding, then, is a means of developing your **value proposition**, which can be defined as the most compelling benefits that attract people to take a desired action (not merely possessing something different for the sheer sake of being different).

In the case of personal branding, the desired action might be getting an interview or a job offer. But there is a longer-term value involved here as well. A clear value proposition will serve you well beyond securing an entry-level career opportunity and can in fact sustain you along your professional journey to greatness. Think about it: even entrepreneurs and other self-employed professionals must constantly persuade their potential buyers of their value.

Here's the bottom line: a well-conceived value proposition can help in climbing the ladder within an organization if managers and executives can be made to see and understand your unique contributions.

News Flash #3: Most People Don't Think This Way

Yes, you have competition. Luckily for you, most of them are not serious threats to your personal brand because they don't think in the terms you are now exploring.

Why? Most people simply do not think to apply branding principles to themselves or their own situation and therefore do a mediocre job at best of marketing their professional identity—if they market it at all. Given that reality, simply by applying strategic thinking to career planning, job search, personal branding, and career management, you will gain a distinct advantage over many others who are more task oriented (e.g., "I have to create a résumé," or "I must apply for five jobs today").

Although there are no definitive statistics on the application of strategic planning principles to personal development, it is widely believed that only a small percentage of people formally establish goals. Estimates on the percentage of goal setters vary, ranging from three percent to 20%. The exact percentage is unimportant; the point is that most people do not have a strategy for positioning and developing their personal brand.

If being among a small percentage of people who manage their personal brand is not strong enough motivation to actively build and manage your personal brand, consider more tangible payoffs. Merely being "in the club" of personal brands will not set you apart from your competition. However, personal branding practices like defining your value proposition and knowing how to communicate it in a cover letter can elevate your job candidacy into the top two percent of job seekers, according to career expert Evelyn Salvador.[5]

How? Again, the primary reason is because most of the other 98 % of job and opportunity seekers are not managing their professional career as a brand.

Personal Branding Simplified

So how do you get to the point of owning and operating a personal brand that will set you apart from the competition?

Well, by picking up this book, you have taken a big step in that direction. And mind you, there are many other books, blogs, and podcasts that promote personal branding as a strategy for managing your professional persona. You are well on your way!

Published works on personal branding are often impassioned pleas by authors to adopt a personal branding mindset. What is usually missing, though, is how to get there.

For example, personal branding experts give advice like "clearly articulate your value proposition" and "cultivate your network of contacts." Sounds good, but what do they mean and how do you do those things?

Realizing that personal branding is a key to professional success is indeed an important first step. And hopefully by now you are convinced of its potential power in your professional life. But it is another matter entirely to then go forth and apply a usable framework to build, maintain, and grow your personal brand.

That's what we'll do over the course of this book. Our focus will be on taking a series of clear steps in the personal branding process.

In a nutshell, the careful development of a personal branding strategy can be reduced to three key pieces we'll call the "3 Ms" of personal branding:

- *Meaning.* Understanding the purpose, values, and mission that guide what you do;
- *Makeup.* Combining traits, talents, skills, training, and attitude that are potential sources of value for the people that you serve, and;
- *Message.* Communicating your brand through face-to-face interactions and online presences.

Create and manage your personal brand by focusing on these three areas. Do so in this specific order.

First, Meaning must be clear to *you*; after all, it is your brand! Nothing else, including the other two personal branding dimensions of Makeup and Message, are relevant without first having Meaning in your life that is known and lived on a daily basis.

Makeup then plays off of Meaning; it is the knowledge and skills needed to compete in your chosen field. These can only be rightly determined once Meaning is recognized.

Finally, Message is all about communication. Think about it, though. You will have no idea what the relevant brand messages about you should be unless Meaning and Makeup are already clear and present in your mind. Only then can a Message be transformed from words on paper into daily actions.

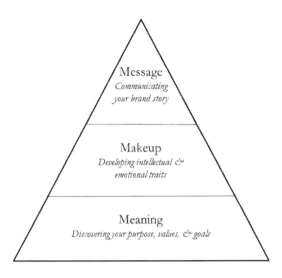

Figure 1.1 - Dimensions of a Personal Brand

Take Action

Ask yourself these important questions before we proceed with the process of building your personal brand.

1. Using a 7-point scale, with 1 being "very unimportant" and 7 being "very important," rate the importance of personal branding in achieving career success in the field in which you work or plan to work. Why did you assign that rating?

2. Of the three dimensions of a personal brand (Meaning, Makeup, and Message), which one do you believe will require the most work on your part over the next three months to develop? Why?

3. Identify a person who works in the profession or field in which you work or plan to work who possesses an admirable personal brand. What are the characteristics or qualities of that person that positively influence their personal brand?

A Dream Job

To land your dream job, you should know what you want to do and what you'd be great at. It's one of the most important decisions of your life! What type of job should you pursue? Does the job you think you want align with your interests? Can you clearly articulate your strengths, task preferences, interests, and motivations?

What's Included in This Package

An interactive online tool that shows you over 650 careers ranked according to your likes and dislikes. You'll be able to sort careers by education levels, search for enjoyment levels related to specific careers or explore what you'd like or dislike about specific careers. You will also have insight to your greatest strengths and your career development path based on preferences, interests and motivations.

Take Action: Self-Assess NOW http://bit.ly/SelfAssessME

2.

DEBUNKING PERSONAL BRANDING MYTHS

"Other people's beliefs may be myths, but not mine."
—Mason Cooley, aphorist

Now that you know what a personal brand is and have a plan to develop one, it might also be helpful to also understand what it is not.

Many different perspectives exist on personal branding. Unfortunately, not all of them offer accurate views.

Some misunderstandings about personal branding lead to cynicism and perceptions that it is a self-centered, self-serving mindset. If true, the negative takes on personal branding would be justified... but they are not.

The following five "myths" must therefore be addressed before we proceed any further with learning how to build a personal brand.

Myth #1: Personal Branding is Bragging

Some people are reluctant to embrace personal branding because the idea of promoting their abilities and performance runs counter to their modest nature, or sounds (to them) too much like "tooting their own horn."

Yes, promotion is part of personal branding; but a great brand's true value resides in the product itself and the benefits of the product to users—not in the bluster.

Promotion is simply how we effectively communicate our brand's Meaning and Makeup to the world. In order to truly resonate, that messaging needs to be real, relevant and heard.

Baseball Hall of Fame pitcher Dizzy Dean was once asked how many games he thought that he and his brother, Paul, who was also a pitcher for the St. Louis Cardinals, would win during the upcoming 1934 season. Dizzy Dean predicted 45 games combined and went on to say "it ain't bragging if you can back it up." The brothers went on to win 49 games between them that season, and the Cardinals won the World Series.[1] Dizzy

Dean wasn't bragging—his message simply related the value he and his brother could bring to the team.

Personal branding is not bragging; it is backing up your Meaning and Makeup while communicating your value.

Another characteristic of great brands that serves to debunk the myth that personal branding equals braggadocio is that the value delivered by great brands often results from first *listening* to the community around them.

For salespeople, it is often assumed that traits like assertiveness and confidence are the most important attributes leading to their success. While these traits are valuable in a profession where the word "no" has deflated many a salesperson, empathy and concern for others are equally or more important. Said another way, projecting a desirable brand identity is not just about what you say; perceptions of your brand are also influenced by what you believe and the actions that arise from your beliefs.

Leadership expert John Maxwell says "people don't care about how much you know until they know how much you care." This idea has great significance for building a personal brand. While what you know is important (your Makeup is indeed part of the value you offer to other people), your brand's value to others increases exponentially when they believe that your brand does something for *them*.

As such, practicing "look at me" personal branding, intentionally or unintentionally, is incompatible with building a brand grounded in serving others.

Myth #2: Personal Branding = Your Social Media Presence

Personal branding first appeared on the scene in the late 1990s. Management expert Tom Peters' article "The Brand Called You" published in business magazine *Fast Company*, served as a call to take advantage of the new tools of the day—the World Wide Web and email— to communicate the value and character of your brand.

In the years since Tom Peters introduced personal branding into the vocabulary of business professionals, ease of communication using social media channels has lowered the barriers to entry in launching one's personal brand online. The popularity of social networking sites is a reflection of how individuals have taken to social media to express their personalities and ideas. Consider the number of active users on the most popular social networking sites:

- Facebook – 1.1 billion active monthly users
- YouTube – 1 billion unique monthly visitors
- Twitter – 288 million active monthly users
- LinkedIn – 200 million members
- Google+ – 359 million active monthly users.[2]

The global reach of these and other social networking sites has taken Tom Peters' view of personal branding and amplified it. A person with modest technology skills can now easily create a strong presence on social media sites.

The huge user numbers on major social networking sites can easily lead people into thinking that social media is the one and only key to personal branding success. It is not! Social media is a communication channel—nothing more. We can tirelessly work to post updates on Facebook, send tweets on Twitter, make connections on LinkedIn, and so on and so forth; but those efforts represent only a small part of the overall management of a personal brand.

Social media must certainly play a major role in the implementation of the Message dimension of your personal brand. However, your brand is more than just the words you say and images you share through social media.

Remember, a personal brand is a process for identifying, developing, and communicating your unique value. The "identifying" and "developing" have to happen before there is anything to "communicate!" Thus, personal branding is by necessity more than one's social media presence. As a result, you can have a brand without using social media, but you cannot communicate using social media independently of your brand.

Myth #3: Personal Branding is Only for Celebrities

You may have heard of personal branding but dismissed it because you believed it only mattered to celebrities and other high-profile people who need to be ever-aware and highly concerned with the brand image and reputation they are projecting to the masses (and their fans). Think again.

Without question, celebrities in entertainment, sports, politics, business, and other fields routinely use personal branding to remain in constant touch and communication with their followers. Doing so serves as a primary means to maintain their status as opinion leaders, or someone the masses turn to for advice and information.[3]

Let's face it: celebrities, deserved or undeserved, often perform in the role of opinion leaders in modern culture. Consider that entertainment icons like Oprah Winfrey and Ellen DeGeneres are well known for influencing their audiences by recommending specific brands or other products. From 1996 to 2011, Oprah's Book Club featured 70 different books—59 of which reached the top 10 of the *USA Today* Best Selling Books list.[4]

Social media has now given opinion leaders in the "offline world" another channel for exerting their influence. In May 2013, for instance, at the tender age of 82, billionaire investor Warren Buffett joined Twitter (@WarrenBuffett). His arrival on Twitter was greeted by the addition of 1,000 followers *per minute* during the first hour following his first published tweet.[5] Buffett quickly built a following of half a million people on Twitter (even though he proceeded to tweet just three times in the first two months in that space).

You and I may never experience adding 1,000 followers a minute like Warren Buffett did, but that does not mean that personal branding (through social media or any other means) is only to be practiced by people with high visibility in the marketplace. Remember, most people who have popular social brands already had well known personal brands. Social media (a form of messaging) did not make them popular; their personal brands instead were built on their Meaning and Makeup.

So, for example, pop star Justin Timberlake has more than 23 million fans on Facebook and 22 million followers on Twitter. Why is his brand so strong online? It's because of the value he has offered through his singing, acting, and performing over nearly 20 years in the entertainment business (not to mention he is an interesting follow on social media).

Social media has elevated the stature of personal brands like Justin Timberlake because fans and admirers can connect with him, and, importantly, also with other people who share an affinity for him. But without first having defined his purpose (Meaning) and working on honing his craft as an entertainer (Makeup), Justin Timberlake would not be the social media powerhouse that he is currently. The cart did not come before the horse!

You are capable of taking a similar (albeit likely less astronomical) route. The same formula for personal branding used by celebrities (Meaning + Makeup + Message) is precisely how non-celebrities build personal brands, too.

Myth #4: Personal Branding Requires You to Act Differently

The prospect of having to "act" like a brand is unsettling to many people. Their thinking when first presented with the idea of personal branding is often something like "I'm a person, not a pair of jeans!"

They're missing the point. Your brand is who you are and what you bring to the table, not something new or external that you make up and present as your real substance.

Putting personal branding concepts into practice can also be particularly challenging for people without prior marketing knowledge. It stands to reason that a marketing student could more easily be convinced than a student graduating with a degree in chemistry that applying principles learned in his or her marketing courses could be used to also managing a career.

Regardless of one's college major or profession, though, the concept of personal branding has been known to repel certain people whose perception is that creating a personal brand will require them to act out of character. Thoughts like "putting on airs," being a "phony," or coming off as "arrogant" may cross the minds of those who believe that personal branding requires us to maintain a persona different from who we really are.

Let's go to the product brand world to debunk this myth. Figure 2.1 lists *Fortune* magazine's Most Admired Brands list. The companies on this list share one trait in common that we can learn from when building our personal brands: They are all *authentic*.

You cannot fake authenticity! Building a great brand is not about coming up with a clever slogan or tagline, creating eye-catching brochures, or designing a slick website. Great brands make promises to customers and then deliver on those promises! These brands enjoy a reputation for being remarkably consistent—they back up the promises they make.

1. Apple
2. Google
3. Amazon.com
4. Coca-Cola
5. Starbucks
6. IBM
7. Southwest
8. Berkshire Hathaway
9. Walt Disney
10. FedEx

Figure 2.1 - World's Most Admired Companies

Source: "World's Most Admired Companies" (2013), n.d., retrieved from: http://money.cnn.com/magazines/fortune/most-admired/.

Do they fail sometimes? Of course they do. Even when a customer service failure occurs, though, these companies work hard to recover from those failures and restore customer trust in their brand.

What does this mean for you and your personal brand? Contrary to the myth that personal branding will require you to act differently, you *must* in fact act like yourself—be authentic—if you are ever to achieve a successful personal brand! Your Meaning and Makeup represent who you are, so position them to tell the story of your unique value.

Myth #5: Personal Branding is All About Appearances

A brand is a multi-dimensional concept, with one dimension being its observable characteristics or features. Product and service brands therefore use tactics such as logos, color schemes, slogans, distinctive packaging designs, unique fonts, and even brand characters (like the Geico Gecko or Tony the Tiger) to strengthen people's association with their brands.

These tactics help establish a mental connection between a brand as observed by the senses and its Meaning and Makeup. For example, when one sees the golden arches symbol synonymous with McDonald's, it triggers brand associations like "fast food," "American culture," "value prices," and other thoughts, favorable or unfavorable, held in memory.

Likewise, similar tactics can be used to associate your personal brand with who you are and what you represent. Your appearance, business cards, wardrobe, and résumé are just a few examples of the observable characteristics or features you use (whether you are presently conscious of it or not) to communicate your personal brand.

Here's the problem. There is a tendency to put too much emphasis on these outward expressions of a personal brand at the expense of a person's real Meaning and Makeup. For example, an advice article titled "5 Components of an Awesome Personal Brand" listed the following elements as essential to a personal brand:

- A central hub such as a website to house and showcase information
- A professional photo
- A catchy tagline
- An interesting biography
- Consistent social profiles.[6]

These tactics are certainly complementary parts of your Message strategy. However, the overt focus on Message elements by personal branding "gurus" is troubling. Their advice either assumes your Meaning and Makeup are clearly developed and on permanent display or simply ignores their primary importance in building and delivering a winning personal brand.

History can be an effective teacher, and history offers many examples that debunk the myth of personal branding being all about appearances. For instance, remember the late 1990s? The period known as the "Dot-Com Bubble?" In the late 1990s, the commercial Internet began to grow and created opportunities to develop online business models. Entrepreneurs did just that, attracting great interest from investors seeking to profit from the Internet's growth. But by 2001, many dot-com companies were going bankrupt, having burned through their investment capital while making little or no profits.

One reason some companies failed was that they spent excessively on marketing, attempting to use Message in the same way far more established and popular brands such as Coca-Cola and Chevrolet used it. The

23

difference between dot-com brands and established brands, though, was that the established brands enjoyed the benefits of decades of marketing and personal brand establishment. They did not buy their exposure overnight. Rather, they bask in the payoff of years of delivering value to customers through their products and advertising. Their Message has Meaning and Makeup behind it. Unfortunately, marketers at companies such as Pets.com and Toys.com thought that if only they could build up their appearances quickly they would gain customers and success.

The same cautionary tale can be told to those of us engaging in personal branding. You cannot build your personal brand quickly. It takes persistent work to uncover your Meaning, refine your Makeup, and then share your Message.

Take Action

Ask yourself these important questions before we proceed with the process of building your personal brand.

1. Which myth of personal branding would be most likely to hold you back from adopting a personal branding mindset? Why is this myth an obstacle? How can you overcome it?

2. Can you think of a celebrity or other high-profile person whose personal brand you admire? Which element or elements of that personal brand (Meaning, Makeup, Message) do you find strong or admirable?

3.

BRANDING BOOT CAMP

"If this business were to be split up, I would be glad to take the brands, trademarks, and goodwill, and you could have all the bricks and mortar—and I would fare better than you."

—John Stuart, former chairman, Quaker Oats

What Exactly Are You Marketing?

If you have any uncertainty about what exactly is being marketed through the practice of marketing, John Stuart (quoted above) offers the answer. We market brands, which are representations of products, services, and ideas—essentially the value that we offer to meet the needs of others.

Where did the concept of branding start? Various accounts of the history of branding place its origins anywhere from 400 to 4,000 years ago. What's not in dispute is that branding was born out of the necessity to put identifying marks on one's livestock to indicate ownership.

How does that historical origin tie in to modern day branding? The marketing use of brands has a similar purpose, with a widely accepted definition of a brand being the use of a name, term, design, symbol, or any other feature to uniquely identify a seller's product in order to distinguish it from other sellers.[1]

Today, though, brands have evolved far beyond their original purpose of simply being identification marks.

Brands build up value in the minds and hearts of people who come in contact with them through usage, advertising, or the influence and input of other people. How people respond to brands influences behaviors (think brand loyalty) and leads to recommendations to friends (or, these days, the posting of positive product reviews online). It's a feeling, an association that grows from meeting and exceeding expectations, or of doing what you said you were going to do, and prioritizing the customer experience.

Your brand is the most valuable asset you can develop to begin to truly advance your professional career at a pace commensurate with your innate abilities and ambitions. But you must first have a firm grasp on the fundamentals of traditional branding in order to begin the process of developing your personal brand.

Two words in the previous sentence are crucial to your understanding of branding:

- "Process." Personal branding involves a series of steps that move you through understanding and building from your Meaning, Makeup, and Message. It is not one thing you do; personal branding requires completing many tasks needed to implement the three dimensions of your personal brand.
- "Begin." While there is a definitive beginning to personal branding, there is no definitive ending. In other words, your brand is always being impacted by what you believe, think, say, and do.

Crafting your personal brand is an ongoing process—you will never completely mark it off of your "To Do" list. If that is hard to accept, think about product brands. They are always "on." Similarly, there are no breaks or days off when it comes to marketing your personal brand.

Do not interpret this to mean you will never get a day off if you adopt a personal brand mindset. What it means is that you must be constantly mindful that your brand is being observed, experienced, and evaluated in the marketplace by the people who come in contact with you. Always and everywhere.

You may already be quite familiar with the branding concepts explained in this chapter, or, alternately, brands and brand management may be new ground for you. Regardless of your experience or education with branding, use this information to help you prepare to build your personal brand as an asset that captures the unique value you offer.

What is a Brand?

Although brands may have originated out of a simple need to identify the owner or maker of an object or product, their role in marketing today has greatly expanded. Instead of being a single-dimension concept, brands now fulfill four key roles or value-added functions:

- Brands communicate identity
- Brands project an image
- Brands make and fulfill promises
- Brands engage with individuals and groups to form relationships.

Returning to the definition of a brand given earlier, the default role of a brand is to communicate identity (think brand name and logo). However, to build a distinctive personal brand, the other three roles your brand serves must also be discovered and defined.

Begin now by taking inventory of where your brand is for each of these four roles. Later, consider how you want these roles to be defined as you go through the process of determining Meaning, Makeup, and Message for your brand. Here's a prediction: it is likely that you will change the current state of one or more of these brand roles to get to a state consistent with the goals you now have for your personal brand.

Brand = Identity

As stated previously, brands are usually thought of in terms of the use of a name, term, design, symbol, or any other feature to uniquely identify a seller's product.

In personal branding, your name is your brand. Be proud of it and use it to your advantage. Legendary self-improvement expert and author Dale Carnegie powerfully captured the significance of a name when he said that "a person's name is to that person the sweetest and most important sound in any language."[2]

In the same vein, brand elements such as the name, logo, and colors of a company or organization oftentimes serve as mental shortcuts that immediately associate a product with its owner. No wonder those individuals with an unusual or distinctive name are at a distinct advantage when it comes to nailing down the identity dimension of one's personal brand.

If you have a common name or a name you feel is not distinctive enough, you might honestly consider researching what is required to legally change your name! For example, a LinkedIn search of the name Michael Johnson returns more than 26,000 results (Michael—if you are reading this, do not worry, this is not a deal breaker to building your personal

ME

brand. You can do this!). Fortunately, not all 26,000 Michael Johnsons compete in the same industry or for the same audience.

A less aggressive approach to ramping up your identity specifically as it is associated with your brand name could include differentiating yourself from the pack by beginning to employ the use of your middle initial, by employing a nickname (if you have one that positively reflects your personality), or even by creating something visual like a logo that appears with your name to bolster your messaging (e.g., on business cards, in your Twitter background, and/or on your blog).

Identity elements are important because they can play a key role in creating brand awareness among the audience you are targeting. In the case of a personal brand, the use of your name and visual associations such as a logo and colors not only create an identity for you, but the identity serves to set your brand apart from others against whom you compete.

Even your wardrobe can be used as a differentiator when developing your identity. For many years, IBM employees were associated with a distinctive identity: dark suits, white dress shirts, and red ties. This "IBM look" is often recommended by experts giving advice on how to dress for interviews. Why? It is a distinctive appearance that can set a job applicant or anyone trying to "win business" apart from their competition at first glance. So while we have all heard the adage "don't judge a book by its cover," we also realize that we inevitably form lasting impressions about a person within the first few seconds of meeting them.

Brand = Image

Another role a brand serves is as a representation of thoughts or mental associations that people hold for an object or person, which is **brand image**.

One definition of brand image is a "customer or user experience represented by images and ideas."[3] What that means is that the thoughts and perceptions that one has for a person or object, known as **brand associations**, influence the perceived image.

Formation of brand associations that comprise image does not require product ownership or usage. For example, you likely have perceptions of brands such as Lexus, Taco Bell, and American Eagle regardless of whether you have ever bought or used their products. Similarly, you may not realize it, but people who come into contact with you (or are part of your target market) have associations that relate to you that already shape their image of your brand.

This is yet another reason why branding requires you to always be "on." Actions and behaviors are always being observed by others and play a crucial part in forming perceptions of your brand. We can unintentionally send negative brand messages if we are inconsistent in how we project our brand in the various environments in which we interact with others, be it work, school, church, or social groups, etc.

This dilemma illustrates the difference between brand image and brand identity. **Brand image** resides in the minds of others; the audience that you interact with determines image through the perceptions they hold of you. Those perceptions can be based on past experiences with you, existing knowledge about you, and/or knowledge obtained from other sources, including your social media profiles.

Brand identity, by comparison, is comprised of associations that a brand owner aspires to project or communicate to the target market. Identity represents how you as the Chief Marketing Officer of "Brand You" seek to have your brand perceived.

For virtually every brand, a gap exists between brand identity and brand image. As such, a salesperson who has desired associations like "excellence," "innovative" and "high quality" may find it difficult to succeed in building brand identity if people's perceptions of him or the company he represents are based on a history of mediocre performance, managerial missteps, or other negative associations.

The identity-image gap is a situation of bad news, good news. The bad news is that public perceptions that influence brand image may be inconsistent with associations the brand aspires to maintain, or, worse, are simply inaccurate or untrue perceptions. The good news? The seemingly never-ending task of aligning image and identity can be accomplished through a commitment to building and managing your personal brand.

Even the most admired and successful brands constantly manage brand identity to maintain their standing among consumers. Managing the image-identity gap is another reason why personal branding must be embraced as an ongoing process. There will always be work to do to influence people's perceptions of your brand.

There will always be work to do to narrow the gap between image and identity. That work is the process of personal branding!

Brand = Promises

Brands represent a promise of action that will benefit a customer. People value brands because they stand for intent to deliver value.

Promises made by brands can be explicit or implicit. **Explicit promises** are statements of action, such as a guarantee. Performance standards must be spelled out and then it is up to the brand to meet those stated standards.

Perhaps a more important role brands play is the **implicit promises** they make to the customer. Think of an implied promise as reducing all of a brand's attributes, benefits, ad slogans, and brand associations to a single claim that sets it apart from other brands.

Some of the most successful global brands have risen to their lofty status in part because they deliver effectively on just such an implied promise. For FedEx, the promise is "timely delivery;" for Starbucks, it is "moments of daily inspiration;" for Apple, it is "simplicity."[4] These brands are considered great because their promises matter to consumers, and because as companies they are diligent and exceptional at fulfilling their promises through product innovation, designing great customer experiences, and connecting their brands with their customers' lifestyles.

In other words, delivering on brand promises creates value for those people who interact with your brand.

Understanding that a brand is a set of promises is absolutely essential if you ever expect to build your personal brand. Some personal brand promises are explicit, such as you meeting (and even exceeding) your commitments. Simple actions such as having a report ready by your boss's 5:00 pm deadline or volunteering to help set up a room for a meeting communicate your brand's value in an explicit manner. Implied personal brand promises take on arguably greater significance through developing brand associations that give meaning to a brand. Promises are highly correlated with brand identity (how we desire to be perceived). Thus, coming up with implied promises you want to convey through your brand is important for positioning the unique value your brand possesses.

If you are fuzzy on what it means for your personal brand to be a set of promises, former Starbucks and Lego creative executive Stanley Hainsworth offered a relatable way to look at brand-as-promise when he stated "What is it that you would hope family, friends and strangers would say about you after they meet you or are with you?"[5] The wisdom of asking that question is that delivering on our promises is highly influential in determining the meaning our brand has for others.

> *Explicit promises* are made through what we say.
> *Implicit promises* are made through what we do.

Brand = Relationship

Exchanges between buyers and sellers may be business relationships, but one's decision to buy from a business is often guided by the same criteria applied to personal relationships.

Think about it: an individual may choose friends or associates based on whether or not he or she believes a person can be trusted. Also, the likeability of that person can influence a decision to forge a friendship. Similarly, consumers tend to enter into business relationships with companies and brands that they trust, like, or perceive to be similar to them.

Most of our relationships with brands are discretionary. We have a choice whether to wear Nike or Reebok, eat at Burger King or Wendy's, and so forth and so on. For many individuals, a brand is more than a name and an image; it is like a trusted friend that can be relied upon to deliver value through consistent quality or enjoyable experiences. Whether you realize it or not, brands are often thought of in terms of personality traits (e.g., dependable, caring, friendly) that attract individuals to engage in personal relationships.

Managing your personal brand as a connector is vital to establishing relationships with clients, colleagues, and community. Perhaps the most important personal branding tactic for managing the relationships around your brand is networking. The term networking may not be clear when you are given advice to "build a network of contacts" or "network with others." This uncertainty about networking can result in paralysis, or not building your brand through networking because of the ambiguity of what you should be doing.

Let's clear the air—networking can be reduced to three words: "building good relationships."[6] Whether it is done face-to-face or online, the aim of networking is to begin to build relationships with people who have shared interests for potential long-term mutual benefit.

The four roles of a brand—identity, image, promises, and relationship—are complementary pieces of a personal brand. If any one of these cornerstones is weak, the strength of your personal brand will be limited. To manage your brand means to manage these four roles.

What Brands Do

Building a brand is work that is never completely finished. The fact that branding is an ongoing process should not discourage you from managing your professional life as a brand, though. Quite the contrary.

Any skepticism about the benefits of personal branding can be addressed by asking the classic question "what's in it for me?" The answers should inspire you. Although great brands are remarkable because they are *not* about the brand owner as much as having an outward focus on customers and community, understanding the personal benefits that a well-developed personal brand can have for you can absolutely serve as added motivation to embrace the role of Chief Marketing Officer for "Brand You."

Three ways that actively managing your personal brand will provide benefits include:

- It provides cues about brand values and quality.
- It expresses brand personality.
- It tells unique stories that are your life experiences.

Your brand either possesses these traits or not. Which state do you prefer?

Provide Cues

One way in which brands benefit us is that they serve as mental shortcuts, providing signals about what to think about a product, company, or person when encountered. Think about product brands that possess distinctive cues:

- Michelin = Safety
- BMW = High performance
- Campbell's Soup = Good-for-you food.

We glean a great deal from these small bits of information, using cues like these to make broader judgments about the quality and capabilities of brands. Likewise, building a personal brand is about creating personal brand cues that immediately connect your professional brand with a desirable trait.

For example, Gordon Graham is a professional writer known as "That White Paper Guy," a reference to the genre of research report writing that he does. Graham has earned this brand association by having written more than 170 white papers for business-to-business technology companies.[7] Of course, many professional writers write white papers, but Gordon Graham owns a distinctive position among these writers in the minds of the clients for whom white papers get written. To them, he's "the authority."

You may not have reached a point in your career where you are considered an authority or even commonly known for a particular skill or ability. That doesn't mean you cannot start to use personal branding to develop cues associated with your brand. The reason brands like Michelin, BMW, and Campbell's Soup have consistent positive cues is their product performance sends immediate signals of the value these brands possess.

In the same way, your actions and habits can serve as cues to others encountering your brand that signal what they should think about you. Seemingly simple behaviors like arriving to work and meetings on time, always meeting deadlines, and volunteering to help with projects (none of which require special experience or skill) can create cues such as "dependable" and "focused."

Wouldn't you rather have colleagues describe you to managers who have not met you using terms like these rather than terms like "indifferent" or "inexperienced?" Use your brand to send positive signals.

Express Personality

In addition to sending immediate associations via cues, brands can be developed to immediately project personality traits.

33

This characteristic of branding, which sometimes involves associating inanimate objects with a person's personality, is almost awkward for some people to embrace. How can something that is not a living being (like a hammer or an auto insurance policy) have a personality?

The answer is actually quite simple: We associate human personality traits with objects and intangibles. So a home cleaning product is considered powerful on stains while an insurance company is analogous to a sturdy rock.

A study of brand personality traits found that a vast majority of brands are described by one of five personality dimensions:

- Sincerity
- Excitement
- Competence
- Sophistication
- Ruggedness.[8]

Do those descriptors sound familiar? They should because we use similar language to describe the people that we encounter! Brand personality characteristics are powerful because they can trigger emotion-based responses that affect how we feel about something or someone. When coupled with cognitive cues (thoughts), a distinctive brand personality elevates a brand as the target market forms a deeper meaning of that brand in terms of what to think of it (cues) and how to feel about it (personality).

In contrast, a brand without a distinctive personality may not stir interest among people, not because it is a bad brand, but because of the absence of defined personality traits or story cues to associate with the brand. Projecting a distinctive personality holds even greater significance in personal branding than it does for products or services. Why? Because you *are* the brand, putting the "person" in brand personality.

Personal interaction is very influential in forming business relationships. Even when one company is buying from another company, the transaction is usually carried out by people representing each firm. Human nature is to prefer to do business with companies (and their employees) that are trusted and liked. These are emotion-based states that can be influenced by how our personality is being perceived.

While demonstrating knowledge and ability is important for building favorable brand associations, be careful not to bury your positive personality traits under an "all business" persona. Do you have a hobby? Don't keep it a secret. If you are a Civil War history buff and enjoy participating in re-enactments, share that interest with others. Did you just attend your 35th Dave Matthews Band concert (as a friend of Don's has done)? Share that! Other people will no doubt find these pursuits fascinating (or curious, at the least). It puts a face to a name and differentiates you from all others. It's perhaps memorable or offers a connection point (or just something funny) that the new relationship can exist on possibly for a long time. Your interests are like a window into your personality. Don't pull the shade down!

Tell Unique Stories

Along these same lines, all brands share the characteristic of possessing unique stories, which provide a colorful backdrop for a brand's existence, its successes and failures, and how it connects with people who come into contact with it. A distinctive brand story is powerful in that it can create brand awareness, differentiate a brand from its direct competition, and build customer loyalty.

Think about brands that have risen to cultural icon status. It is not because of reaching a certain dollar level in sales (people don't really follow that information that closely), it is because they have stories that people find interesting or worthy of association.

If you haven't heard it before, the inspiration for creating Starbucks is a very powerful story. Starbucks CEO Howard Schultz fell in love with the coffeehouse concept on a trip to Italy in 1983. He wanted to bring that experience back to the United States and give people a place to gather for conversation and to be a part of a community of people who appreciated that similar experience. Schultz was so inspired in fact that he opened his own coffeehouse, Il Giornale. A few years later, he bought a small coffeehouse chain called Starbucks. Today, Starbucks has more than 18,000 stores in 62 countries.[9]

Starbucks is a great brand not only because it has great products but because it also has a brand story that resonates with people. It's an example of how brand storytelling is a key element in the growth of product brands.

Brand storytelling may be even more relevant in personal branding. Why? Your brand is defined by the stories that you have lived. What you have done, who you have known, and how you have handled life situations have shaped your personality, character, and achievements. It has set you apart and made you distinct.

In the first class meeting of any course I (Don) teach, I ask students to write down an interesting fact about themselves. To me, this is the beginnings of their brand story. Occasionally, a student will respond with a statement like "There is nothing about me that is interesting." That response is wrong and a harmful attitude. It is wrong because unless you have lived alone on a deserted island for years, you have likely had experiences or events that others would find interesting (For that matter, if you have lived on a deserted island for years, you probably have a ton of interesting stories!).

Here's the bottom line: if you are ineffective at communicating your brand story, you will be at a competitive disadvantage with people who are able to transform their personal experiences into compelling brand stories, be it while trying to land a client, secure a job, or gain opportunity anywhere in the business world.

Take Action

Ask yourself these important questions before we proceed with the process of building your personal brand.

1. What are three words that you believe other people would have as brand associations for you? What are three words that you believe are your brand associations? If there is a difference between how you believe others perceive you and the brand associations you identified, explain why you believe "gaps" exist.

2. A brand conveys promises to others. Some are explicit (such as guarantees) while others are implicit (promises based on people's experiences with a brand). State an implicit brand promise you want other people to have based on their interactions with you? Are you currently able to deliver on this promise? If no, what changes are needed to make you capable of fulfilling the implicit promises you aspire to make?

3. Everyone has unique stories that reveal their character and personality. Think of a story about something that has happened to you in the past year. What part or parts of the story (a problem, struggle, or resolution) could be used to tell the story of your brand (your image or promises) that would help make your brand more distinctive in the eyes of others?

Branding Boot Camp

Building a personal brand is about creating personal brand cues about your strengths or capabilities. So where do you start? How do you begin to articulate your personal brand cues and express your distinctive characteristics?

What's Included in This Package

Your Greatest Strengths and Career Development Reports identify the "cues" about your strengths and distinctive characteristics. These reports describe your key strengths in detail and provide single words that describe you. You'll get a jumpstart for creating your personal brand cues.

Take Action: Self-Assess NOW **http://bit.ly/SelfAssessME**

PART TWO:
MEANING—
WHO YOU ARE

4.

PURPOSE

"Definiteness of purpose is the starting point of all achievement."
—W. Clement Stone, businessman and author

Now that you have accepted the job of managing the world's most important brand (you!), it's time to get to work. The question now is "Where do I begin?"

Branding is an ongoing process, but it begins with clarifying your purpose, which can be defined as the contribution or added value you offer to others.

Define it! By doing so, you will project a helpful image to others and also add value to your own life by creating (perhaps once and for all) a deep sense of meaning that brings you the personal fulfillment, joy, and satisfaction you have always wanted.

Creating this positive impact both for others and simultaneously for yourself is one of the great payoffs for defining your distinctive personal brand. To get there, though, you must first figure out your purpose. Said another way, what is your reason for existing?

Drivers of Purpose

Simply put, purpose answers the question "Who am I?"

Now, you need to be careful how you respond. Avoid defining yourself strictly in terms of your profession or work with statements such as "I am an accountant," or "I want to be an emergency nurse." Such labels merely describe jobs or occupations, not purpose.

There is certainly nothing wrong with being a nurse or a teacher. However, your purpose is more likely found *in the meaning and impact that arises from your work or occupation*. So, for instance, a nurse might be better described as someone who helps people heal or get back on track in their lives. Similarly, a teacher might be better defined as someone who inspires others or who helps others discover their own meaning and purpose in life.

Once you truly understand the value you deliver (and also internalize how that valuable contribution feeds your own needs and wants), the work of personal branding (i.e., acquiring the Makeup needed to achieve the desired impact and using Message to communicate your value) becomes a far less daunting challenge. Know thyself!

Purpose is the key to answering the question "Who am I?" So what is your purpose? Self-reflection in two areas—values and motivation—offers the clearest path to achieving clarity about your purpose.

Values

The starting point for understanding your purpose is to identify the core values that guide your thoughts and actions.

Values are the principles that motivate the decisions you make. Like a compass, values provide direction as you make judgment calls about what is important to you (and unimportant), what is right (and wrong), and what brings you happiness (versus produces unhappiness).

Making decisions in alignment with your personal values affects the outcome of virtually every major life decision you make. Whether it is the city you choose to live in, the friends with whom you choose to spend your time, or the partner or spouse you commit to long term, your personal values steer those decisions. The consequences in play here are steep. In most instances, dissatisfaction or unhappiness with any of these decisions can usually be traced back to a choice made in misalignment with one's core values.

Career choice is among the major life decisions that must be made with careful consideration of personal values. After all, you are choosing how and where to invest the bulk of your physical, mental, and creative energy! You want to feel that you are committing your professional efforts to an organization that emphasizes principles and values in alignment with your own core values, not ones that are incongruent with them.

Examine how or even if your core principles match up with those of an organization by considering these four categories of career values:

Intrinsic values. These motivate engagement in activities because you find them interesting or enjoyable (examples include feelings of independence or of making a difference).

Work content values. These include specific tasks performed on a job that are enjoyable or which play to your strengths (such as problem solving, serving others, and/or flexing your creativity).

Work environment values. These entail working conditions that create a positive work setting (such as opportunities to learn, generous benefits, and/or fair compensation).

Work relationship values. Characteristics of these include interactions that matter to you (such as open communication, teamwork, and diversity), all of which are weighed in determining the fit of a career or employer.[1]

Notice that who or what has control over outcomes are different for each of these four career values categories. Intrinsic values are yours, meaning no one else dictates what is important to you except you. Work content values, by contrast, are inherent to a particular job and can connect with your intrinsic values. So, for example, a career as a copywriter responsible for creating content for web pages and social media might be appealing to one type of person because of the variety in assignments involved and the challenge of meeting tight deadlines in completing client projects. That same environment, though, could be anathema to a different type of person with a different brand and a different purpose.

Work environment and work relationship values are influenced by a particular organization's culture, which is comprised of shared values, beliefs, and behavioral expectations among the organization's members. Organizational culture can either mesh with or run counter to an employee's intrinsic and work content values. So, extending the above example, the copywriter who places great emphasis on using his or her creativity to solve a client's marketing needs (a work content value) will no doubt feel that his or her value is not being fulfilled if their ideas are frequently rejected under the mantra of "that's not how we do things around here."

Because work environment and work relationship values are influenced heavily by organizational culture, it can be difficult to determine how well your personal values match with a particular company. However, there are ways to effectively investigate an organization's culture when researching prospective employers.

Indicators of a company's values include:

Mission statement. Does the company's marketing or internal communications material contain a statement about values? Many organizations even go beyond a mission statement and elaborate on the organization's values. If these exist, how closely do the organization's mission and values match with the values that are important to you?

Philanthropy. What social causes or nonprofit organizations does this particular company support? Corporate philanthropy is rightly interpreted as a statement of a company's values and priorities.

Physical environment. If you have an opportunity to visit an organization's facilities or offices, are there visible cues about its culture and values? One indicator is the layout of work spaces. Is it a maze of cubicles isolating workers from one another? Or an open layout promoting interaction and community among employees?

Employee impressions. To learn about an organization's values, go to the information sources embedded there: the employees. Ask them about their daily work experiences through questions such as: "What attracted you to this company and has it turned out to be what you expected?" and "What do you like most about working for this company?" Their stories will either resonate with you and affirm that what you seek in a workplace environment is available there or, alternately, raise red flags about potential conflicts as they relate to organizational values.

> *Values represent what is important to you. Your challenge is to find happiness in the mix of intrinsic, work content, work environment, and work relationship values.*

Motivation

To answer the question "Who am I?" it is perhaps helpful to start by posing a broader query—"*Why* am I who I am?" This question is not intended sound overly philosophical. By contrast, it addresses motivations for wanting to create the personal brand you aspire to possess.

Psychologists have studied motivation extensively but its meaning can really be boiled down to this simple description: moved to do something.[2]

If you consider every decision you make in your life, it can be connected to a motive.

Think about it. You might be seeking an outcome that gives you feelings like pleasure or accomplishment, such as a personal best time in a 5K run, or getting a job interview with the top company on your target list. Alternately, you might be seeking an outcome that avoids guilt or punishment, such as preparing for a group presentation to avoid looking incompetent or arriving at work on time so your boss does not fire you.

Motivations, whether positive and negative, do indeed spur action, create urgency to get things done, and keep you on track toward reaching a goal. To identify and understand what motivates you to fulfill your purpose in ways that align with personal values, you must first determine the sources of energy that inspire or prompt you to get things done.

These energy sources are better known as *extrinsic motivation* and *intrinsic motivation*. One source is not necessarily better than the other; they are simply two different ways that energize you to action.

First, let's elaborate on extrinsic motivation. When actions are guided by the expectation of an outcome separate from the action, extrinsic motivation is what is spurring us to pursue the outcome.

In this scenario, actions are motivated by what is anticipated will occur as a result of the actions. Extrinsic motivation is effective, then, when it is believed that we have some control over an outcome.

For example, a prime extrinsic motivator in business is that being a productive employee will lead to opportunities for pay raises and promotions. The outcomes (raises and promotions) spur action (greater effort or commitment).

You have likely heard the terms "carrot" and "stick" used in reference to incentivizing engagement in a desired behavior. The carrot is the positive reinforcement or reward if the desired behavior is exhibited. It represents a "goody" that one gets for meeting someone else's expectations. The stick, by contrast, is the negative reinforcement or consequences resulting from failing to meet expected behavior. Use of a stick as a motivator is based on the belief that one will learn from the situation and be motivated to avoid a similar negative result in the future.

Use of a carrot or stick depends on the person or organization holding the power to administer extrinsic motivators. For example, some college professors might provide an incentive (or carrot) for class attendance, such as bonus points that serve as a reward for consistent class attendance. Other professors might take the stick approach to extrinsic motivation for attendance, having a policy of reducing a course grade or employing automatic course failure if students are absent too frequently.

Whether a carrot or stick approach is used, both types of extrinsic motivators are based on the premise that someone else influences your behavior. Because extrinsic motivation is not being driven by your own desires or interests, its potential to effect permanent behavioral change is uncertain at best.

Think about an employee that gets a raise. If their salary increases $150 a month, it may be appreciated. However, will the higher pay motivate him or her to work harder, longer hours, or be more committed to the company? It might at first; but over time, the influence of the pay raise on job-related behaviors likely fades. It's not a matter of the amount of money—your pay could be doubled, but would you double your efforts or commitment?

The point here is that you are unlikely to find your purpose solely through extrinsic motivation.

Next, let's look at intrinsic motivation. While extrinsic motivation can move you to reach goals because of a reward linked to action, your personal brand needs to be guided by a stable internal compass that moves you in the direction of what is important to you regardless of consequences. This internal compass can be described as intrinsic motivation.

In contrast to external motivation, internal motivation occurs when you enjoy rewards from engaging in behaviors you find interesting or enjoyable. Intrinsic rewards don't come from an outside source (e.g., a pay raise at work or a grade on an exam). Instead, you might say that we give intrinsic rewards to ourselves. *You* decide how actions or outcomes are to be valued.

Determining the sources of your intrinsic motivation may seem challenging at first. Ask yourself: what do you truly find interesting or enjoyable?

It must be noted that intrinsic motivation resides not only within an individual, but it exists in the relationship between a person and a task. For example, people are attracted to a hobby more often by intrinsic rewards than external outcomes. So, for instance, an avid fisherman could be drawn to the sport because he enjoys spending time outdoors, or because the act of fishing provides a connection to memories from childhood, or because it is a way to "recharge the batteries" after a hectic week. If you think about it, these outcomes can be experienced regardless of how many fish are caught... even if that number is zero!

Understanding sources of intrinsic motivation is crucial in today's professional work environment. That's because workers are often expected to engage in self-management, using their intelligence and experience to direct their work activities and contribute to organizational goals. Today's professional is called upon to add value by innovating, problem solving, and devising solutions that serve customers and their organizations.[3] Intrinsic motivation, therefore, plays a vital role in career success in that it contributes to personal development, such as enhancing one's levels of high-quality learning and creativity.[4]

These benefits may effectively sell you on the importance of tapping sources of intrinsic motivation. The question may remain, though: how do you find an answer to the question "What do I find enjoyable or interesting?"

The following offers a partial list of intrinsic motivators that may help you better understand your own personal internal drivers of behavior:

- Having a sense of purpose in your job
- Autonomy—being able to make your own decisions
- Feeling a challenge
- Mastering a subject or skill
- Community—making social connections with others
- Recognition and acclaim.[5]

Intrinsic motivators should be weighed along with extrinsic rewards when evaluating career options, as well as specific employment offers from organizations. Of course, compensation can be a strong motivator, just as feelings that you are being unfairly compensated can be an equal and opposite de-motivating force. Once compensation is agreed upon, though (and assuming it is perceived as fair), motivation to manage the day-to-day activities on the job comes primarily from intrinsic sources.[6]

Understanding the internal drivers that are important to you not only can steer you toward the right kind of career but are invaluable when determining the fit or match between you and a prospective employer.

47

Extrinsic Motivation = Influences action because of what it does for you
Intrinsic Motivation = Influences action because of what it does to you

Determining your Purpose

Now that you know more about what values and motivation are, it is time to uncover *your* values and motivation and *your* guiding principles, or what moves you to action. To get to your purpose, you must ask yourself a few key questions—ones that only you can answer.

Career Values assessment. If values represent what is important to you, then asking questions about the importance of outcomes associated with intrinsic, work content, work environment, and work relationship values can give you a glimpse of the type of professional situation you long to find and in which you will flourish. Figure 4.1 contains a self-assessment to identify your priorities that will be influential in selecting a career that is well suited to your purpose

Finally, think about a company or job you are interested in. Based on what you know, how good is the fit, or "match" between your top three career values and the company or job?

Rate each on a scale of 1 to 10, with 1 being a "poor match" and 10 being an "excellent match." After completing the questionnaire and rating the values match, ask yourself, has your opinion of the company or job as a desirable opportunity been confirmed or questioned? Explain.

After completing the career values assessment, review your results in two ways. First, compare importance ratings across career values categories by looking at the average ratings for the intrinsic (seven items), work context (three items), work environment (four items), and work relationships (three items). This comparison provides insight into the relative personal importance of each career values category.

For example, if the average of ratings for intrinsic values is 3.3 and average for work relationships values is 1.7, these results suggest that a career that has personal impact is more desirable to you than one that offers social interaction.

Second, assess the importance of different career values by examining your top three values list. Are they all from the same category? Or do your most important values reflect diversity in priorities?

Instructions: Rate the importance of the following career values using the following scale:

1 = Not Important   2 = Somewhat Important   3 = Important   4 = Very Important

Make a difference to society (I)	Work in a small organization (WE)
Work alone (WR)	Use creativity (WC)
Fast paced environment (WE)	Have friendships with co-workers (WR)
Receive financial rewards (I)	Attain position of power and authority (I)
Solve problems (WC)	Help other people (WC)
Autonomy to prioritize work (I)	Job security (WE)
Work with other people (WR)	Mentor others or be mentored (WR)
Recognition for achievements (I)	Work in a large organization (WE)
Opportunities for growth/development (WE)	Ability to set own work schedule (WE)
Enjoy a work/life balance (I)	Intellectually stimulating (I)

I = Intrinsic Value   WC = Work Context Value   WE = Work Environment Value   WR = Work Relationship Value

Figure 4.1 Career Values Assessment

Let your values priorities serve as your guide in finding a career or company that matches well with what is truly important to you.

Defining your Purpose

Once you are familiar with how values and motivation drive your purpose (and have identified the values most important to your professional existence), the final step is to synthesize this new knowledge by putting your reason for being into words, or "packaging purpose," if you will.

The benefits of distilling your purpose into words are:

It's communicable. Committing your purpose to words is a simple way to convey what drives you to create value for others and yourself.

It's memorable. Putting your purpose into words enables others to easily associate your personal brand with the values and motivation behind your purpose.

It's powerful. Most of your competition has not gone through the process of defining their purpose and writing it out. Articulating your purpose sets you apart by creating clear meaning for your brand.

Still unconvinced about the need to define your purpose? Or unsure you can complete this task? Try one of the two following approaches for transforming why you exist into words. One option is to create a personal purpose statement. Another is to create a seven-word bio. These approaches combine a methodology with creativity, allowing you to follow a "recipe" while also giving you the leeway to package your purpose into a collection of words relevant to you.

Purpose Statement

You are likely familiar with the concept of a mission statement. Most organizations have one in an effort to summarize what they do and who they serve. A mission statement is often described as a statement of a firm's 0reason for being.

Sound familiar? It should be, because the focus in this entire chapter has been on understanding and communicating your own personal reason for being- your mission statement!

Many   branding experts suggest composing a mission statement for your personal brand. It might feel a little weird at first as some people struggle with the idea of applying concepts used on non-living entities like a business to describe themselves. However, the concept of a statement that summarizes your reason for being is absolutely essential to the development of your personal brand.

It might help to think of this exercise less like the development of a mission statement and more like the development of a *purpose* statement. Package thoughts about your existence and value offered in the form of this purpose statement. In contrast to a mission statement that suggests existence is a means to an end, a purpose statement declares who you are and what you have to offer—today, next week, and next year.

Why is defining your purpose preferable to stating a mission? Human resources expert Stephanie Krieg cited three advantages of packaging your personal brand using purpose instead of mission:

- *Purpose plays to the Law of Attraction.* When you state your purpose, it can have the effect of drawing others to you that have a similar vision or interests.

- *Purpose is inspiring.* A purpose energizes you to be and do, while a mission is a course of action we strive to follow to stay "on course."

- *Purpose is empowering for the greater good.* Purpose goes beyond a goal orientation associated with a mission statement. When you are able to live out your purpose, the benefits realized are not only personal but also impact your co-workers, customers, and communities.[7]

The process of writing a purpose statement is similar to earlier tasks you completed in that it will help you to gain a superior understanding of your values and motivations. You need to ask tough questions of yourself to develop the key pieces of your purpose statement because that kind of hard look in the mirror is critical to developing your personal brand!

Three questions that specifically reveal purpose are:

- *Who am I?* To answer this question, consider the industry in which you aspire to belong, the target market you serve, and the type of work that you do. Part of your purpose is wrapped up in these standard descriptions or labels that are applied to your work.

- *What do I do?* This question takes into account tasks performed in your work, how you create value for those you serve, and why your work is valuable to other people.

- *What is my impact?* A follow-up to the "what do I do?" question is "so what?" Impact answers the "so what" question, meaning what benefits are realized from what you do? How does the work that you do differentiate you?

Let's put these three pieces together in a template you can use to write your personal purpose statement:

I, (your name), am (description of industry, occupation, market served, or job title) that (value created and benefit).

Using this template, I (Don) created my own personal purpose statement:

I, Don Roy, am a marketing educator who helps position future businesspeople by encouraging them to grow intellectually and compete professionally.

After writing this statement, I reflected on it to consider if it truly fit me, or if it was simply a collection of words written to the template. The answer

51

to me is clear—it is indeed me! It is the approach I take in developing the courses I teach, how I conduct each class, and the counsel I give to college students. The elements of my purpose statement figure prominently in the scholarly research I engage in and the professional writing I do.

Seven-Word Bio

If the thought of writing a purpose statement seems too formal, an alternative method for defining your purpose is to condense your reason for being to seven words.

Creativity expert and author Todd Henry says a seven-word bio is useful for self-definition because it forces you to clarify what you want to do or accomplish, not just describe yourself by occupation or job. Another benefit of a seven-word bio is that it communicates your values and motivation to other people more clearly and quickly than a long, drawn-out description based on professional or job labels.[8]

In a crowded market in which there are many brands (both products and people), getting attention and being noticed can be greatly enhanced by utilizing the simplicity of a seven-word bio to increase the chances that the distinctiveness of your purpose will stand out. The process for crafting your seven-word bio will be similar to how you go about developing a purpose statement. The questions asked in that exercise (Who am I? What do I do? What is my impact?) are equally applicable when attempting to arrive at your seven-word bio.

That's not to say this is an easy process. You will likely go through several versions—some using eight words, some using five—and that's a good start. Keep writing and revising until you arrive at that magical seven-word bio that nicely sums up your purpose.

I (Don) subscribe to the "practice what you preach" philosophy. Writing a seven-word bio is no exception. So, after several iterations of stating my purpose in seven words, I came up with the following bio:

"Develops knowledge and creativity in future businesspeople."

When I reviewed how well this statement matches my purpose by comparing it to my career values and motivation, I determined that the statement well fits my purpose as a college professor training marketing students.

Take Action

Before moving to the next chapter, let's review the following highlights for consideration as you take steps toward the final development of your personal brand:

1. Think about the categories of career values—intrinsic, work context, work environment, and work relationship. Which values category is most important to you as in meeting the needs of a certain career or employer? Why?

2. Consider the two sources of motivation—extrinsic and intrinsic. What role do you envision extrinsic motivation playing in the construction of your personal brand? What will be the role of intrinsic motivation? Which source do you believe will have more influence on your professional growth and development? Why?

3. Which of the two methods for defining purpose—a personal purpose statement or a seven-word bio—do you favor for use in your personal branding efforts? Why? Have you completed this assignment? If you do not like either method, how would you go about defining your purpose utilizing a different method?

Purpose

Understanding what's important to you and what will bring you satisfaction in the workplace is vital in your professional fulfillment. Examining your career values prior to taking a job will help you find the right job that aligns with your purpose and will allow you to flourish.

What's Included in This Package:

Your Greatest Strengths Report will help you understand your "work content values," and Your Engagement & Retention Report will help you understand and articulate your "work environment values." Both reports will help define your purpose.

Take Action: Self-Assess NOW **http://bit.ly/SelfAssessME**

5.

PASSION

"Vocation is the place where your deep gladness meets the world's deep need."
—Frederick Buecher, author and theologian

Purpose defines your reason for being. When applied to managing your professional identity like a brand, purpose serves a similar role to that of a mission statement for an organization, providing meaning that guides the career you pursue, the employer you choose, and your actions on the job.

There's another force that guides development of your personal brand's Meaning, though: Passion. In contrast to the thought-provoking questions used to clarify your purpose, passion is stoked by emotions. Feelings you have about what you do and the impact you create through your work comprise your passion.

Where exactly does passion fit in with building your personal brand? There are many differing opinions about this question. One view is that passion should dictate your career choices, or what type of job to hold, what company to join (or whether or not you should go out on your own as a freelancer or entrepreneur), and what city to live in as you pursue your career goals. A different view is that allowing passion (as opposed to logic or realism) to steer your career planning could result in a person going down a professional path that does not yield the fulfillment and happiness desired.

What Is Passion, and What Should I Do with it?

Before you can know whether or not you should allow your passion to lead in your personal brand development, it's worthwhile to examine exactly what passion means.

Passion for most people is defined as eliciting strong emotional responses such as excitement or love. However, the origin of the word passion can actually be traced to the Latin root "pasi," which means "to suffer."

Whoa! Does this mean that you should be searching for a job or employer that will make you suffer? Of course not. A deeper interpretation of passion in the context of "suffering" is that your passion is linked to something for which you are willing to invest your time and effort heavily, and yes, even suffer through occasional adversity and disappointment in order to pursue. It is precisely because of the intense emotional connection you have with something you are passionate about that you are willing to endure tough times in order to eventually enjoy the pleasure and satisfaction derived from the endeavor!

Think of passion as the fuel for your purpose. Your values and motivation are energized when connected with passion.

In the context of personal branding, passion can be defined as the sources of happiness that energizes the work you do. The impact of passion is not confined simply to carrying out your professional job duties. Is evident in the volunteer work you perform, the topics of conversation you choose to engage in on social media, and the hobbies or outside interests you enjoy. All of these non-professional pursuits in which you exhibit your passion speak volumes in defining your personal brand. As such, recognizing your passion is vital to personal branding success. The challenge is how to channel passion to strengthen your personal brand while also enjoying the synergy of a career in which your passion figures prominently in your work.

Follow Your Passion

A line of advice that has become quite popular in recent years is to "follow your passion" and select a career that allows you to do something you enjoy. This philosophy is a distinct departure from the advice of old to judiciously and logically evaluate career options using hard criteria such as pay, opportunities for advancement, and prestige.

You have no doubt also heard references to "starving artists," or people who do what they love and are skilled at without regard for the reality that the financial compensation for doing what they love or are skilled at doing is low, unsteady, or even uncertain.

A clear trend in the U.S. economy and workforce has been the emergence of the "creative class," or workers who add value to society not through traditional worker attributes but rather through their creative output. Scientists, teachers, artists, engineers, healthcare professionals, business people, and more comprise this group of creatives (no, it's not just poets and musicians) that are innovating every day in an effort to offer solutions and add value.[1]

The rise of the creative class has helped to break assumptions that career success and opportunities to enjoy extrinsic rewards such as high salaries are limited only to more standard "professional" occupations, or people who eschewed career paths steered by mantras such as "follow your passion."

The follow-your-passion bandwagon is driven by people who espouse ideas like these:

"Choose a job you love, and you will never have to work a day in your life." —Confucius

"Do what you love and the money will follow." —Oprah Winfrey

At the heart of advice taken from Chinese philosopher Confucius, pop culture icon Oprah, and others like them who subscribe to the "follow your passion" philosophy is that doing so has benefits that will enable you to find happiness and satisfaction in your work. Among the payoffs of following your passion to guide your career planning are:

- You can relate more to the work, sparking greater creativity.
- Work does not feel forced upon you because it does not really feel like work.
- You will get greater fulfillment when you achieve success.[2]

Build your personal brand through a career that follows your passion. Why? Because your work will consume a significant amount of your life, so you might as well spend that time doing something you love! And, as Oprah said, the money will follow!

An excellent example of how following your passion can influence personal brand and Meaning can be found in the story of Kevin Carroll. Carroll was abandoned by his parents as a child and raised by his grandmother. His escape from life's difficulties was the playground. It was a place where his feelings of shame and doubt disappeared, as well as where he discovered his athletic gifts.

Carroll's love of sports eventually led him to study sports medicine and become an athletic trainer. His relentless pursuit of his passion eventually landed him a job as head trainer of the Philadelphia 76ers professional basketball team.

Being one of only 30 or so head trainers of a professional basketball squad in America could easily be interpreted as reaching the pinnacle of career success; but there was more awaiting Kevin Carroll. He later joined sports apparel juggernaut Nike in a corporate leadership role and today is an author, speaker, and consultant who focuses on how sport can empower young people around the world to find their passion.

Carroll describes one's passion as an individual's "red rubber ball." For Carroll, the red rubber ball is a symbol of play. It is what inspired and excited him. It was his passion, and by following it, he achieved great things, arguably never working a day in his life (and, yes, the money and prestige followed). His story well illustrates how passion serves as the greatest guide in the development of a personal brand.

Whatever You Do, Don't Follow Your Passion

Before you start chasing your red rubber ball and following your passion to build a career, though, here's a word of warning that many people you encounter will offer: Don't do it.

That is not my advice; but it is a view held by many career and personal branding experts.

One of the most vocal opponents of the follow-your-passion mantra is Cal Newport, a computer science professor at Georgetown University, who has researched the relationship between passion and career selection. In a nutshell, Newport says the suggestion to follow your passion is "terrible advice."

What's his reasoning? One reason is that following your passion to (eventual) success can be difficult to do. For instance, most people do not have a pre-formed passion that can be easily translated into a career. Newport advocates looking to intrinsic motivators (e.g., autonomy and creativity, as discussed in Chapter 4) for inspiration in connecting passion to work.[3]

So which road is better for you? One factor to help you determine whether following your passion is the route you personally need to take to build a personal brand is a variation on the chicken-and-egg argument — namely, does passion create great work, or does great work create passion?

Proponents of following your passion believe it is the former, and that passion fuels creativity, innovation, and persistence to grow. In contrast, skeptics of the follow-your-passion approach believe that career passion is an output rather than an input.

Newport says passion must be earned and that it is a benefit realized from developing a skill that is highly valued. Instead of trying to follow a passion, Newport advocates that we should develop it.[4] Only then, he says, can "following" it yield professional dividends.

Finding passion (and in turn, Meaning) in your personal brand through the skills you work hard to develop is rightly considered to be the preferred path to long-term career fulfillment. Monique Valcour, a professor who researches careers, says that following passion is insufficient for creating a sustainable career, one in which you will be challenged to develop skills and add new ones.[5]

So like the skilled craftsman whose commitment to learning a craft shows in works of exceptional quality while exhibiting a genuine passion through output, infusing your own personal brand with passion is best achieved by working constantly to become competent and skilled to a level that what you do is highly valued (i.e., people will pay for what you do).

Here's the bottom line: Having passion for something isn't enough. You must put in the work, too!

Authenticity: Passion's GPS

How do you know when you have found the passion that drives your personal brand and are willing to work incessantly on that passion to produce personal branding results?

You know that passion is fueling your purpose when you are able to observe consistent behaviors and actions in your work as well as through interactions with others. That consistency also plays out in terms of being the same person across different life contexts, whether they take shape at home, school, work, or social situations.

Essentially, you have arrived when you cannot nor need not turn your brand on and off dependent on your environment.

This state of consistency is perhaps best defined as authenticity, which has been described as the "moral inner voice" that develops from our experience.[6]

Authenticity is an admired characteristic in corporate brands and personal brands alike. That's because when we encounter authentic brands, we feel assured that "what we see is what we get."

An authentic brand does not hide its true character behind mission statements or slogans; instead, its actions follow beliefs.

So, what does it *really* mean to be authentic? And how do you develop that moral inner voice that aligns daily performance with principles? Some personal branding advocates mistakenly equate authenticity with simply "being ourselves." That works just as long as who you are is who you want to be! By contrast, marketing expert Seth Godin believes authenticity is based on doing what you promise, not "being who you are."[7]

Marc Ecko, a pharmacy school dropout turned celebrated fashion entrepreneur, has built a billion-dollar business through a focus on brand authenticity. Ecko has three criteria for assessing the authenticity of his personal brand:

1. How truthful am I to myself and others?
2. What is the emotional impact that can be made on others through actions?
3. How flexible I am to change?[8]

In a nutshell, authenticity is not just a buzz word. It is essential to maintaining the integrity of your brand.

Creativity expert and author Todd Henry says "you cannot sustain yourself long-term on the approval of others."[9] You cannot keep up with fulfilling promises that are not in line with your personal values.

Barriers to Authenticity

If finding your authentic personal brand is intimidating, take heart — that is a very normal feeling! Determining and maintaining the principles and actions that guide how your brand develops and evolves is complicated by barriers that cloud the picture of brand authenticity.

Think of it this way. The three greatest obstacles to finding your moral inner voice are beliefs, fear, and social influences.

Beliefs. Actions are rooted in beliefs. What you think about yourself and the world around you influences how your personal brand is perceived… for better or for worse.

The brain is like a computer, operated by "programming" that gives the body instructions on what to think, feel, and do. Beliefs are the program code, and if your personal brand has "bugs" in it and is not projecting an authentic brand, it is likely that reprogramming is needed to change the beliefs that are held.

You are probably familiar with some of these beliefs that contribute to corrupt brand programming:

- "I don't have enough experience."
- "You have to know someone to get ahead in this field."
- "I am too young (or too old)."
- "I don't have anything unique to offer."
- "I lack the education or training needed to succeed."

We could go on and on, but you get the picture. Limiting beliefs like these threaten authenticity because they discourage you from even trying to find your inner voice. "Why bother?" the inner voice asks. "The odds are stacked against you."

Reprogramming faulty beliefs like those in pursuit of an authentic personal brand requires two things: 1) separating valid beliefs from perceptions that are convenient excuses for why you cannot achieve more, and; 2) replacing the flawed code with beliefs that are consistent with your purpose.

Now, mind you, some limiting beliefs are valid – like run away as fast as you can from people who proclaim "you can do anything you want to do!" That said, *you can do most anything better and at a higher level of performance than you are currently exhibiting* if you are able to connect beliefs with your purpose and get to work fueling your passion!

For example, when I (Don) first considered going to graduate school to become a college professor, I started by reading the requirements to earn a Ph.D. As I read the requirements, I realized limiting beliefs were trying to control my thoughts. Initial responses went something like this:

61

- Pass a written comprehensive exam? *That will be hard.*
- Pass an oral exam in front of faculty? *They will crush me.*
- Complete a dissertation research project? *I could never do that.*

How did I overcome those limiting thoughts? I focused instead on the truth that if I wanted to be a college professor and fulfill what I saw as my purpose —to help prepare future business professionals —I would have to reach these three milestones. A clear purpose made the difference for me in applying for and eventually earning a Ph.D. degree. However, to act on my purpose, I had to first reprogram certain beliefs that resulted in greater authenticity for my personal brand.

Fear. Similar to limiting beliefs about the capabilities needed to develop a personal brand that aligns purpose with passion, fear is a self-imposed roadblock to authenticity. Fear is an emotional state that is a reaction to negative thoughts and beliefs.

In the context of your professional career, fear could be triggered by anxieties such as that you will struggle to find a job, will be unable to meet your boss's expectations, will not be accepted by your peers, or other negative outcomes that are incompatible with the vision of your personal brand growth.

The grip that fear can have on responses to a situation is a formidable obstacle. Just think about how the body handles fear by manifesting in elevated heart rate, sweaty palms, and even withdrawing from the world around you. These are ways that fear takes control!

A quest for personal brand authenticity requires you to understand and embrace fear. Yes, to triumph over fear you must do just that!

One way to filter fear out of your personal brand is to recognize that most fears do not actually exist. Perhaps you have heard that fear is not an emotion but rather an acrostic that stands for:

False
Evidence
Appearing
Real

In other words, the fear that you possess often comes from inaccurate perceptions about the world around you.

Consider a common fear many young professionals have early in their career —feelings of inadequacy because they do not know as much as their more senior colleagues. The false evidence in this situation is that a person one year out of college should not compare his or her knowledge base to a colleague with 12 years or even two years of experience. Guess what? Your senior colleagues did not start out as skilled and confident as they seem today (false evidence)! They learned too and failed (and grew), just as you will!

We are not suggesting that you simply pretend you have no fears. In fact, how you respond to and overcome fear could become an essential part of the narrative of your brand story. Having fear makes you human; how you overcome fear can be the difference between finding your authentic personal brand and being constrained by limiting assumptions about what you can be, do, and have.

Social influences. The quest to develop and communicate your authenticity can be complicated by challenges from people and situations that are at odds with your purpose. For example, a distinguishing characteristic of social media is that you can not only demonstrate knowledge and skill, but you also can give others that have never met you a glimpse into your personality via your sense of humor, outlook on life, and how you handle the ups and downs of the day.

One way in which social pressures could hinder authenticity, though, is feeling that you need to conform in some way by using a certain style of humor, taking a position on an issue that is popular with a peer group, or otherwise acting to please people in your social circles. Of course, that does not fit the definition of being authentic by expressing your moral inner voice. In sharp contrast, that would be expressing someone else's voice!

A second threat to your brand authenticity posed by social influences is blandness. It is possible to be so protective of your brand messaging through what you say and what you do that you succeed in not alienating or offending anyone... but you also do not resonate or connect with people, either!

Like product brands, a personal brand will not be universally accepted and "bought." You will have detractors, particularly when you allow your authenticity to be evident in your work. The expression "haters gonna hate" applies here. Having non-fans is normal; be more concerned if you do not alienate anyone because it means your authenticity has not made others around you the least bit uncomfortable!

It is important that you do not mistake being authentic with being perfect. While it is important to be a caretaker of your brand's image, accept that it will get "dinged" at some point.

Perhaps it is an error of omission, such as missing an important project deadline. Or, your brand might take a hit from an error of commission if you post a joke on Twitter that turns out to be offensive to others. Either way, imperfection is reality —you are going to screw up sooner or later. Luckily, authenticity actually acknowledges imperfection rather than trying to mask it or pretend it does not apply to us.

Authenticity is appreciated not because you are "being real" but because your actions are driven by your personal values.

Take Action

1. Applying the definition of passion as "sources of happiness that energize the work that you do," identify a task (e.g., solving problems) or cause (e.g., teaching children to read) for which you are passionate. What characteristics of the task or cause would you find enjoyable if they were part of your "day job?" Why?

2. What role do you see passion having in your professional career? Should you follow your passion to find a satisfying career, or do you expect passion to arise from commitment to become skilled and experienced in a particular field or profession? Why do you feel this way?

3. Consider each of the three barriers to brand authenticity—beliefs, fear, and social influences. For each barrier, assign a rating for the significance of the threat on a scale of 1 to 10 with 1 representing "no threat at all" and 10 representing "very much a threat." Why did you assign the rating that you gave? For each threat, identify actions you can take to reduce the chances of it affecting the authenticity of your personal brand.

Passion

Knowing that passion is stoked by emotions, consider the importance of being self-aware of your emotions and understanding how to develop your emotions to guide you to passion. Finding passion through emotions will guide you to long term career fulfillment.

What's Included in This Package

An analysis and development plan around your self-motivation and self-management behavior. This analysis will help you understand how you respond to situations and the impact that your emotions can have on others.

Take Action: Self-Assess NOW **http://bit.ly/SelfAssessME**

6.

SNAPSHOT – SITUATION ANALYSIS

"It pays to plan ahead. It wasn't raining when Noah built the ark."
—Anonymous

Taking a Snapshot

Once you have gained clarity on your purpose and passion, the next step toward defining Meaning in your personal brand is to begin the task of charting a course for your future.

Before you can set goals for your professional brand and career, it is necessary to take inventory of what is happening with you and the world around you. In strategic business planning, this process is referred to as conducting a situation analysis.

What that means is that managers cannot make decisions on a course of action to take in the future without first understanding what is happening right now. Doing otherwise (e.g., making plans for the future without assessing present circumstances and characteristics and how they could impact future decisions positively or negatively) would be considered generally unwise or, worse, risky.

A fitting analogy for what a situation analysis does is that it takes a snapshot—a current representation of someone or something at a particular point in time. A snapshot captures attributes or characteristics of an object or person. Similarly, a situation analysis done in personal brand planning summarizes your attributes and puts them in the context of the environment around you (i.e. trends and market circumstances, such as employment opportunities).

In this chapter, you'll learn how to take a "career selfie," or personal snapshot, that elucidates all the factors that can impact your professional brand. More importantly, you will become more confident in taking the next step of interpreting your snapshot to find personal brand Meaning.

Developing Your Snapshot

The process for developing your personal brand snapshot is based on a business planning tool that has been used since the 1960s: SWOT analysis. SWOT is an acronym that stands for strengths, weaknesses, opportunities, and threats. The scenery that makes up your personal brand snapshot is comprised of attributes and characteristics in these four areas.

The four elements of SWOT can be reduced to two factors based on where they are controlled: internal factors and external factors.

Internal Factors

What are the characteristics and traits that describe you and represent who you are at the time of a snapshot?

These characteristics represent the internal aspect of your personal brand. You are who you are—the good, the bad, and the ugly—as represented by your attributes. They are specific to you, not controlled by the government, your parents, your boss, or anyone else. That, however, is good news because if you are dissatisfied with the appearance of the internal aspect of your personal brand snapshot, you have the power to make changes.

It is no different than if you looked at a snapshot of yourself and decided you did not like the look of your hairstyle or felt you should lose 10 pounds. You could then set to the task of changing your hairstyle or making necessary changes to shed the extra weight.

Likewise, if you find certain aspects of your snapshot favorable, you can seek to use these attributes to your advantage. So, for instance, if you took a snapshot of yourself minus your glasses and liked your appearance, you could switch to contact lenses and feel more confident about your physical appearance.

These analogies to personal appearance highlight that internal factors considered when conducting a situation analysis can be categorized as strengths (positives) or weaknesses (negatives).

Strengths. A logical starting point for developing your personal brand snapshot is to identify the strengths you possess. These are the abilities, traits, competencies, and skills that you have acquired or developed. The strengths you possess are unique to you. Yes, others might share your

68

ability to solve problems or create blogs using WordPress, but these strengths are attributed to your efforts to learn, improve, and apply yourself.

Where do you look to identify strengths? You can seek out objective evidence of your strengths from sources such as:

- Observations people make about your personality.
- What you learn about yourself when successfully handling difficult situations.
- Feedback from a boss or teacher.
- Certifications or training earned.
- Recognitions or awards received.

Look for evidence from these five areas to pinpoint your positive attributes. For example, your friends might compliment you on being a great listener, or for being there for them when they have problems. Similarly, your supervisor might praise you for empathy exhibited when serving customers. Taken together, these two pieces of evidence would suggest that interpersonal communication, particularly being an effective listener, is one of your top strengths.

In addition to identifying strengths based on gathering evidence, quantitative assessments have been developed that give insight into one's strengths. There are far too many strengths assessments to discuss them all here, but some of the most established ones include:

- *Clifton StrengthsFinder.* This assessment categorizes personal strengths into 34 themes based on responses to a 177-item instrument. Some of the personal themes include Analytical, Connectedness, Futuristic, Harmony, and Relator. There is a cost to take the assessment, or you can gain access to it by purchasing the book *StrengthsFinder 2.0.* More information can be found at https://www.gallupstrengthscenter.com/.

- *.Myers-Briggs Type Indicator.* A classic assessment for identify personality types, the Myers-Briggs personality framework consists of 16 types based on four personality dimensions: Introversion-extroversion (preference for inner world with self or outer world among others); sensing-intuition (how information is processed); thinking-feeling (influence on decision making); and judging-perceiving (responding to stimuli from the outside world). The cost to take the MBTI is around $150, and you receive detailed feedback on results of your personality type. Free tests based on the Myers-Briggs framework are an alternative and can be found online. Visit http://www.myersbriggs.org/ to learn more.

- -*Strong Interest Inventory*. Responses to this 291-item instrument are used to identify one's strengths among six general occupational themes: realistic, investigative, artistic, social, enterprising, and conventional. The Strong Interest Inventory can be applied to situation analysis by matching the theme that best characterizes you with the environment of a particular job (e.g., organization culture and co-workers' personalities). This assessment is used by people at a variety of life stages, including high school students trying to find a college major, career exploration by college students, and professionals considering career changes. Learn more about the Strong Interest Inventory at https://www.cpp.com/products/strong/index.aspx.

- *Kolbe A Index*. In contrast to assessments of personality and cognitive abilities, the Kolbe Index assesses one's strengths with regard to behavior. The 36-item instrument yields four "action modes" that guide behavior: Fact finder. follow thru. quick start. and implementor. Findings related to these action modes reveal whether you are more inclined to take action to prevent problems or initiate solutions. Results from the Kolbe A Index do not indicate good or bad traits but simply give insight into how your instincts can influence problem solving. Find out more at http://www.kolbe.com/assessments/kolbe-a-index.

The four strengths assessments shared here are not meant to be endorsements or recommendations. They are simply among the best-known assessments and are based on rigorous development and validation. Regardless of whether you select one of these assessments or find another one elsewhere, make the decision to invest in yourself by diving deeper into understanding your strengths.

Weaknesses. A realistic snapshot of your personal brand must include an acknowledgement of weaknesses. Period.

One of the most challenging aspects of conducting a situation analysis, whether it is for a business or your own brand, is to be brutally honest in your assessment. Without question, it is not much fun to point out your own weaknesses. However, in order to truly understand your limitations and plan for future growth, it is essential to call out yourself by identifying weaknesses.

Uncovering your shortcomings can be done in a similar manner to how you built a list of strengths—namely through observation by others, self-reflection on a situation in which you did not enjoy the desired outcome, and/or feedback from a superior or mentor.

The responses you get back may be tough to digest. For instance, it may be painful to acknowledge that you were passed over for a job or promotion because of perceptions that you do not pay close attention to details. Whether true or not, if that is how you are perceived, then it is a weakness to address. Perception is reality, as the saying goes.

The good news about the set of weaknesses you possess is that a weakness is typically not a permanent condition. A weakness can often be overcome once it is recognized in the first place!

Taking a personal snapshot using SWOT analysis will spotlight weaknesses to be aware of and to go to work on. It is then up to you regarding how you proceed. Will you attempt to improve in areas that are weaknesses so that they are no longer weaknesses or even become strengths? Or will you choose to avoid careers or professional situations/opportunities that expose your weaknesses and potentially harm your performance?

External Factors

While strengths and weaknesses are characteristics of your personal brand snapshot that uniquely define you at the time of taking the snapshot, opportunities and threats are occurrences in the external environment that are generally beyond the control of a person.

External factors are faced by all members of a particular group or industry because of the fact that these developments take place in the world around you. Your analysis of external factors will lead you categorize them as opportunities or threats to your personal brand.

Opportunities. Positive trends or events in the external environment can be opportunities that you can pursue for growth and advancement. Keep in mind, though, that because they are external, opportunities do not only hold potential for you but for others like you as well.

For example, a trend in the field of marketing is that many companies are focusing more on creating and publishing brand-related content such as blogs, videos, brochures, and web pages. Someone has to create this content, and people trained in creative areas such as writing, photography, graphic design, and videography stand to benefit from this trend. One study found that 54% of firms plan to add content marketing personnel to their marketing team.[1] In this example, recognizing the trend of companies creating more jobs in content marketing could lead you to further explore the types of positions available, salary ranges, industry groups and organizations to follow, and other information sources to learn more about the opportunity.

Threats. Even if you are a "glass half-full" type of person who sees the positive in any situation, a personal brand situation analysis is not complete without identifying potential threats to your professional development. Much like opportunities, threats also exist in the world around you and cannot be stopped or reversed by you or any other individual. Threats that go unrecognized, or worse, ignored, can hinder the launch or growth of your professional career.

An example of how a threat plays a role in personal brand planning is having an awareness of employment opportunities in a geographic area as measured by unemployment rates. If you live in Nevada, for instance, and want to remain there gainfully employed, you would benefit from recognizing that the state's unemployment rate (8%) is second highest in the nation and considerably above the national average of 5.9%.[2] Of course, employment prospects in your chosen field might be better than that for the geographic area overall, but you are nevertheless smart to be aware and remain alert to potential threats by scanning the external environment for this type of information.

Where to Find Opportunities and Threats. In traditional SWOT analysis, five main external factors are examined to determine whether trends or developments are taking place that could impact strategic decisions, either favorably or unfavorably. These five factors can be applied to conducting a situation analysis for a personal brand, too. They are:

- *Socio-demographic trends*: Changes in population, values, lifestyles, and industries that could affect employment opportunities. For example, as Baby Boomers (persons born between 1946 and 1964) transition from the workforce to retirement, the needs of this generational group will change, too, which will affect the types of products and services sought by them.

- *Competition*: In business strategic planning, competition constitutes other businesses vying for the same customers. In personal strategic planning, competition is made up of other people seeking the same career opportunities as you. Competition can be direct (other candidates applying for the same job as you) or indirect (businesses not hiring their own employees and instead outsourcing tasks).

- *Technological change*: Innovations can create demand for specialized labor to implement said innovations, or, alternately, reduce the need for the current labor force by automating certain tasks or processes.

- *Economy*: Changes at macro- or micro- level spending that could either stimulate or reduce the demand for goods and services from a particular industry. A variety of economic indicators exist at national, local, and state levels, by industry, and for consumer behavior.

- *Political, legal, and regulatory climate*: Just as businesses are impacted by laws and regulations that can promote or curtail demand for their products, personal brand planning should include consideration of how laws and regulations can affect an industry or career in which you are interested. For example, passage of the Affordable Care Act is expected to dramatically change the healthcare industry. Will new career opportunities arise from changes in healthcare delivery? A report by the U.S. Department of Labor projects demand for healthcare services and providers will actually rise by 70% by 2020.[3] Changes in government regulation of healthcare, along with an aging population (socio-demographic trend) and innovation in medicine and healthcare services (technology change) are external forces contributing to a changing environment for working in the healthcare industry.

When evaluating how external factors shape the appearance of your personal brand snapshot, you must categorize external issues as either opportunities that could be acted upon for personal gain or threats that could bring harm if unrecognized or ignored.

The way to tell the difference between whether an issue is an internal factor external factor is to ask "If I went away, would the issue go away?" If the answer is yes, then it is an internal characteristic specific to you, and you must determine if it is a strength or weakness. If the issue still existed if you were not in the picture it is external and could represent an opportunity or threat.

Snapshot of Your Personal Brand

Now it is time to take on the role of personal brand photographer, bringing together the various pieces of information needed that form your personal brand snapshot in the form of a SWOT analysis.

In order to compile the information needed to evaluate internal and external factors, use the same technique that you employed to gain insight into your purpose and passion: ask questions. Drill down to understand your own characteristics in terms of strengths, weaknesses, opportunities, and threats. Then, go even further and examine causes and consequences of the characteristics that make up your personal situation analysis.

Know Your Strengths

A starting point for creating your personal brand snapshot is to know the strengths that you possess. Questions to uncover your strengths can be broken down into the following areas:

Tangible strengths. These characteristics relate to observable accomplishments or capabilities, including:

- What education or training experiences do I have?
- What education or training designations or certifications have I earned?
- What are demonstrable skills or abilities that I possess?

Relationships. Take stock of the goodwill you have built up in your personal relationships. The members of your network may be based on personal friendships or virtual interactions such as connections achieved through belonging to a group on LinkedIn. Questions to ask about professional relationships include:

- Who are people that can talk about my strengths (e.g., a former teacher or boss)?
- Who are people in my personal network that could be helpful in making connections or giving advice?
- What organizations do I belong to that promote networking opportunities for members?

Intangible strengths. These positive characteristics are more subjective or cannot be observed directly. Questions include:
- What positive traits do I have?
- What do I do better than others can?
- What strengths do I possess that others see in me?

You may think of other questions that could reveal personal strengths. Regardless of which questions you ask, look to the areas of tangible strengths, relationships, and intangible strengths to reveal positive attributes that potentially give you an advantage in the pursuit of a career or job.

Confront Your Weaknesses

Perhaps the most uncomfortable part of conducting a situation analysis as you develop your personal brand snapshot is to confront the personal shortcomings that could be preventing you from achieving your goals.

75

Possessing weaknesses is nothing to feel shame over. After all, you cannot be outstanding at everything you do! What is unacceptable about weaknesses, however, is refusing to admit they exist. Denial is not a remedy for improvement.

Questions you should ask to pinpoint weaknesses fall under the same three categories as the questions utilized to build your strengths list:

Tangible weaknesses. In what areas are you lacking capabilities or credentials to compete for opportunities in your chosen field? Specifically:

- Do I lack the experience level expected in my field?
- What formal education or credentials do people in my field hold that I do not have? (This question includes your GPA in school and its relative standing with others.)
- Are new skills or technologies being practiced in my field for which I have not been trained?

Relationships. You may realize you have shortcomings in the area of interpersonal relationships that could put you at a disadvantage when competing for a job. Ask yourself:

- What is the quantity (number of contacts) and quality (strength of relationships) of my professional network?
- Is my professional network growing? Or stagnating?
- Am I consistently working to build up both the quantity and quality of my network?
- Do I have high-quality "go to" people in my network who are willing to advocate for me (e.g., write recommendation letters or make introductions to new contacts)?

It is possible that the answers to these questions will actually reveal that you have strengths in relationship building. However, for most of us, particularly early-career professionals, relationships will emerge as an area for improvement.

Intangible weaknesses. This area may be the most difficult in which to uncover weaknesses as they are often revealed only by candid self-assessment or brutal honesty from people who care about you:

- What personal, negative characteristics or traits are observable to others?
- Are there attitudes or behaviors I exhibit that are "turn offs" and that cause people to avoid me?
- What weaknesses or areas for improvement have others shared with me?

It's no fun compiling a list of all the ways you are falling short of who you would like to be, but in order to realize growth in your personal brand, awareness of your weaknesses is essential.

Identify Opportunities

Scanning the external environment to identify opportunities is accomplished by asking questions related to the five external environment factors (socio-demographic trends, competition, technological trends, economy, and political/legal/regulatory climate). Questions may relate to an industry or organization that you are interested in pursuing, or they could relate to a geographic area that interests you as a place to live.

Examples of questions you could ask to identify opportunities include:

- Which cities or states are rated as top destinations for young professionals? (Socio-demographic trends)
- Are there forecasted changes in population characteristics that will increase demand for products and services in a particular field or industry over the next 5-10 years? (Socio-demographic trends)
- Which industries, companies, or cities are most challenged to attract employees? (Competition)
- Are there new technologies emerging in the industry? (Technological trends)
- Are their certain skills or competencies that are growing in demand in my field? (Technological trends)
- What is the growth rate of the industry in which I want to work? (Economy)
-What state and local taxes do residents pay? (Political/legal/regulatory)

The mix of questions you ask from the five types of external factors will depend on the importance that certain criteria has in your career choices. For example, if you are interested in having what is referred to as work-life balance, you may ask more questions pertaining to geographic areas (e.g., availability of recreational activities and demographic makeup of area residents). Alternately, if where you live is less important, the questions you may ask to uncover opportunities will likely be more about the industry or profession you are considering as a career (e.g., growth rate of industry and increased demand for certain skills or abilities).

Acknowledge Threats

The external environment not only holds opportunities that can be acted upon for one's benefit but also poses threats or obstacles to the pursuit of personal brand growth. Questions asked about occurrences in the socio-demographic, competitive, technological, economic, and political/legal/regulatory environment can reveal these threats and how significant of a challenge they pose.

Among questions to ask to determine potential threats are:

- Are there shifts in buyers' needs or wants that could reduce demand for products and services in my chosen industry or profession? (Socio-demographic trend)
- Could population shifts in a city, state, or region in which I am considering living impact employment potential in my industry or profession? (Socio-demographic trend)
- How many new college graduates exist in my field that are coming on to the job market at the same time as I am? (Competition)
- What is the general state of human resource supply and demand for my aspirational profession or job? (Competition)
- Do any technologies or skills for which I am trained risk becoming obsolete or being overtaken by new technologies? (Technological trend)
- How "recession proof" is my chosen industry or profession? Is earning potential and employment security in this field vulnerable to economic downturns? (Economy)

- Are there any current or pending regulations that could negatively affect demand for the job or position I intend to pursue? (Legal/political/regulatory)

Just as confronting weaknesses and admitting shortcomings requires brutal honesty on your part, you must also acknowledge legitimate external threats that could reshape the industry or profession you are targeting. For example, the travel industry was dramatically affected when airlines and hotels began to sell their services directly to travelers online. At the employment peak in the early 1980s, there were more than 46,000 travel agents. Today, that number has dwindled to approximately 13,000.[4] Recognizing shifts in how travel is purchased and adapting services offered to clients in response to those shifts was a way travel agents met the threat head on and learn to survive, innovate, and thrive in business.

After the Snapshot

Use of SWOT analysis as a strategic planning tool tends to focus on construction of "the list." Yes, compiling a list of strengths, weaknesses, and opportunities—as well as threats—is a must if you are ever to understand your current situation.

Perhaps the greatest value of conducting SWOT analysis is gaining a firmer understanding of the significance of the issues on the list. A great deal of thought, reflection, and research are required to answer questions that enable you to develop your personal brand snapshot.

Arguably the greatest weakness of SWOT analysis is that so much effort goes into creating the picture of the current situation that making actionable decisions based on the situation analysis that results gets less attention than it deserves. In short, what do you do with the information you compile from a personal SWOT analysis? The process of laying out strengths, weaknesses, opportunities, and threats can be a pointless exercise unless that information is then utilized to set strategies for advancing your personal brand.

Transforming the list of characteristics in your SWOT analysis into strategic priorities is a two-step process. First, you should realize that not all issues listed in your SWOT analysis carry the same weight or importance in terms of potential impact on your personal brand.

Here is where the "analysis" in situation analysis comes into play. You must categorize each issue as being of low, moderate, or high importance with regard to its potential effect on you. You can even quantify your evaluations by assigning a 1 for low importance, 2 for moderate importance, and 3 for high importance (score weaknesses and threats with negative ratings of -1 for low, -2 for moderate, and -3 for high). Assigning numeric ratings to SWOT characteristics is not an absolute must but it is a way to do a quantitative analysis of your snapshot.

Once SWOT characteristics have been evaluated for their importance, and as potential areas of emphasis emerge from this evaluation, the next step is to look for ways to combine elements from your snapshot to create strategic priorities.

Personal brand growth strategies based on SWOT findings should be guided by the acronym MAC, which stands for *Match*, *Avoid*, and *Convert*.

Match – Strengths with Opportunities

The low hanging fruit that can be picked from SWOT findings is to look for ways to match personal strengths and market opportunities. The Match approach is about taking advantage of what you do well by pursuing opportunities for which your strengths are a good fit.

Review the answers you gave to the questions you asked to identify strengths, then compare your answers to these opportunities identified. Are there clear and evident connections between personal strengths and external environment conditions or trends?

For example, let's say you cited two of your tangible strengths as exceling in mathematics and having solid quantitative skills. Also, your analysis of the external environment uncovered that a significant development in many industries is using "big data" (i.e., massive amounts of customer and market information captured from transactions, online behaviors, and other sources) to make key business decisions.

Applying the Match approach could lead you to see an opportunity to leverage your quantitative strengths and create a plan to position yourself for a career as a business intelligence analyst. Subsequent actions you might take could include learning more about the specific skills and formal education new hires will be expected to possess in that field, as well as industry groups or organizations you could begin to follow or join online, and finally, identifying persons in your professional network that could be helpful in giving advice or making introductions to others in your new chosen space.

Avoid – Weaknesses and Threats

In contrast to the Match approach of playing to your strengths and using them to pursue market opportunities, the Avoid approach recognizes what should *not* be done.

One of the benefits of taking a personal brand snapshot is that it can reveal the true you—blemishes and all. The personal brand snapshot must not be "photoshopped" to mask undesirable attributes and external trends. Doing so could lead you to make decisions that expose your weaknesses or make you vulnerable to negative external market conditions.

Returning to the example of a career as a business intelligence analyst, if you struggled to pass college algebra and do not enjoy working with numbers and data, it does not matter that more than one million jobs related to big data will be added to the U.S. economy by 2020. That's because based on your skill set and passions, you would not be able to compete in that industry… at least based on your current snapshot.[5]

Similarly, the fact that the number of travel agents has shrunk by more than two-thirds in the past three decades (threat) suggests that you should be wary of pursuing a career as a travel agent. Now, given that there are still 13,000 people working as travel agents, career potential obviously still exists. However, aspiring travel agents must clearly size up the situation and realize it could be a challenging climb to break into the industry.

The decision then becomes this: are you willing to assume that risk and commit to building your strengths so that you have a better chance to compete for job opportunities? Or do you apply the Avoid approach and focus your personal strategies in other areas.

Convert – Weaknesses into Strengths

Be careful not to apply the Avoid approach too quickly when evaluating how your weaknesses might hinder certain professional pursuits. Perhaps the best news about your personal brand snapshot is that it is only a temporary representation of "Brand You." Most of the attributes that comprise your strengths and weaknesses can be changed.

81

Just as your appearance in a snapshot can change by donning a new hair style or hair color, via weight loss, or by wearing or not wearing glasses or an updated wardrobe, you can always work on strengthening your attributes—particularly ones that are currently weaknesses.

Compared to Match and Avoid, the Convert approach is riskier to carry out. It does offer great potential, though, for transforming you and growing your personal brand.

For example, if you are one of the millions of people who fear public speaking, you can take steps to become a more confident speaker by reading books on the topic, joining a public speaking group like Toastmasters, attending seminars where input is encouraged, getting coaching on the skill, and/or finding a means to practice the art of public speaking regularly (perhaps at work or even at church). The process might be painful at times and there is no guarantee of success (risk), but a person that breaks out of their shell to become an effective oral communicator often open doors to career opportunities and promotions that flat out never would have occurred if the Convert approach had not been taken.

Take Action

Ask yourself these important questions or take these important actions before we proceed with the process of building your personal brand.

1. Complete a strengths assessment by selecting one of the instruments discussed in this chapter (Clifton StrengthsFinder, Myers-Briggs Type Indicator, Strong Interest Inventory, or Kolbe A Index), or find a similar assessment. Based on findings from your strengths assessment, what are the greatest strengths you possess that could be leveraged in a career or job?

2. Prepare a Personal Brand Snapshot (SWOT Analysis) by reflecting on the strengths, weaknesses, opportunities, and threats questions. After answering the questions, prioritize your findings by assigning an importance rating to each item using a 1 for low importance, 2 for moderate importance, and 3 for high importance.

3. Apply the MAC (Match, Avoid, Convert) approach to your SWOT analysis findings to set three strategy priorities for your personal brand.

Situation Analysis

Are you ready to take your "career selfie"? Understanding the characteristics, strengths and traits that describe you is a great step toward being able to articulate your personal brand and enable you to match yourself with opportunities.

What's Included in This Package

Your Greatest Strengths, Summary & Keywords and Career Development Reports will identify your key strengths, keywords that describe you, your interests, preferences and motivations.

Take Action: Self-Assess NOW **http://bit.ly/SelfAssessME**

7.

SETTING GOALS

"The secret of getting ahead is getting started. The secret of getting started is breaking your complex, overwhelming tasks into small manageable tasks, and then starting on the first one."

—Mark Twain

Begin with the End in Mind

The final step for building your brand's Meaning is to set a course for where you want your personal brand to take you.

Goals are the primary means used to map out growth and development to advance your career and enhance your quality of life.

Two analogies are fitting for the role of goals in self-management. One way to look at goal setting is to understand that goals serve a purpose similar to how you use a map when taking a road trip. If you are driving from Dallas to Denver, you likely would not get in your car and start driving in a general northwest direction. You would instead refer to a map or to GPS to identify the destination and the route needed to get you where you want to go. Similarly, goal setting pinpoints the destination and forces you to think about what you need to accomplish in order to arrive at your desired destination.

Another analogy for how goals are used in personal brand management is the process of writing a story. You have probably watched movies or TV shows in which the opening scenes are actually the end of the story, and subsequently all of the scenes that follow show events that transpire leading back to that foreshadowed conclusion. Think of goals as the conclusion of a story. They are the happy endings you wish to create. Once the desired conclusion is known, you can then create the scenes that build up to that desired ending and successfully achieve your goals.

Setting goals to advance your personal brand is one of the most crucial aspects of managing You, Inc. —the world's most important brand. Three reasons stand out that explain why you should make goal setting a priority.

First, goals align actions with purpose. You have explored your purpose and the passion that fuels it. Setting goals enables you to pursue outcomes that match up with what you want to be, do, or have. Feeling a sense of purpose can inspire you to set goals that bring that purpose to life in your daily activities.

Second, goals give focus to your time and energy. Time is one of the most precious resources you have. However, as we all know, there are always many demands placed on that resource by you and by other people. Goals prioritize those demands, guiding you to spend time on the activities and projects most related to the goals you've set.

Third, goals create a competitive advantage for you. How? Most of your competition (the other professionals vying to build their careers and improve their quality of life too) have not systematically set goals. It is estimated that no more than three percent of Americans have written goals.[1] As such, you can set yourself apart from 97% of the competition simply by buying in to the process of setting goals and writing them out!

Of course, merely setting goals does not lead to success. If it did, a lot more than three percent of the population would be doing it! What leads to success is creating the concluding scenes in your mind as a necessary visualization step toward determining what you need to do to bring those final scenes to life.

What Types of Goals Should You Have?

Perhaps one reason that 97% of the population does not set goals is that it seems like an overwhelming task. How do you decide what your goals will be? How many goals should you have? What separates goals from dreams?

To answer these questions, think about building your personal brand through two different perspectives: life parts and time horizon.

Life Parts

Although the focus of building your personal brand discussed in this book is related to your professional career, do not lose sight of the fact that your time at work is just one component of your life. Americans work an average of 1,790 hours per year, ranking the United States lower than countries like Mexico (2,226 hours) and Russia (2,029) but higher than countries like Canada and Sweden (1,710 and 1,640 hours, respectively).[2]

While Americans work more hours than all but 10 countries globally, your time at work still represents only about 20% of the available hours in a year. Thus, be careful not to set goals related exclusively to your professional growth and development.

To achieve a balance between the work and non-work aspects of your life, look to the following six "life parts" as areas in which to consider setting goals: Career, relationships, wellness, spiritual, financial, and "bucket list."

Career goals. Your commitment to personal branding suggests that you are already thinking about setting goals that deal with career advancement. These goals can involve the industry or company you are targeting as a possible work destination, the progression of jobs or duties you want to experience, projects with which you want to be involved, and/or training or development that will strengthen your skills and make you more "marketable" for promotion.

Relationship goals. Building a personal brand is not a solo voyage. The strength of relationships developed both inside and outside of the workplace will be influential in your growth. Relationship goals inside the workplace could include forming a relationship with a mentor (or, as your career progresses, becoming a mentor yourself), networking within your organization, and/or building a network of contacts in your industry. Relationship goals outside of work pertain to how you spend some of that 80% of your life when you are not at work. This involves nurturing connections with family and friends, whether face-to-face or virtually.

Wellness goals. You will struggle to achieve career and relationship goals if your "machinery" is not in good working order. What this means is that your health and personal wellness are vital to your overall livelihood. A study by the Gallup organization estimates the cost of lost productivity due to work absenteeism for professionals, excluding doctors, nurses, and teachers, is $24.2 billion annually.[3] Now, the occasional sickness and health problem is inevitable, but proactively managing your personal wellness through goals related to exercise and diet can help keep your body performing closer to its peak potential, and keep you on track to reaching your goals.

As a side note, take advantage of the programs many employers offer to assist employees in setting and achieving wellness goals. The scope of services can vary greatly among companies—some may provide access to health care, pharmacy, and exercise facilities on site, while others may provide fewer benefits). For example, SAS, a global software company, has its own fitness center, clinic, pharmacy, incentives for employees to participate in fitness programs, and smoking cessation programs.[4] Smaller organizations may not be able to make the same investments in the wellness of their employee pool that a large company like SAS can make, but they can still create a culture in which personal wellness is valued. Employers large and small recognize that their people cannot deliver on their value proposition when they are not in good physical condition. Likewise, employees need to take full advantage of whatever level of wellness offerings their current company provides.

Spiritual goals. Many people complement mind and body goals with spiritual goals that strive to explore one's inner thoughts and feelings. While the focus of Meaning in a personal branding context relates to finding significance in your professional career and aligning with personal values and passion, setting spiritual goals is another way to find and connect with Meaning. Just as wellness goals strengthen the body, spiritual goals can strengthen an individual's inner fabric. Study, prayer, meditation, and reflection are just a few practices that allow you to examine the spiritual aspects of your life and to renew yourself from within. And, just like wellness goals, one of the primary obstacles to meeting spiritual goals is carving out the precious time in your day to work on *you* instead of working for someone else. Make the time.

Financial goals. Hopefully, your work fulfills a sense of purpose in your life. Aside from that, though, the practical aspect of having a job is that it is a means to achieve financial ends. As a start, compensation from your job provides for your basic existence—a roof over your head, food on the table, and transportation to get to work, make more money, and buy more of those necessities! However, it is likely that you are looking for more in your life than to "just get by." Your choice to read this book is proof of that fact! You no doubt have visions about how you could enhance your quality of life and the quality of life of those around you with an income that gives you greater financial freedom. Financial goals include, but are not limited to:

- Debt reduction—Paying off credit cards or student loans.
- Savings—Establishing an "emergency fund," or systematically putting money in the bank.
- Long-term investments—Committing to regularly fund retirement or education plans.
- Discretionary purchases—Accumulating money for a new car or dream vacation.

As discussed in Chapter 4, money is an extrinsic motivator that could inspire one to perform at a higher level. In the long run, however, money is not as effective as intrinsic motivation (like autonomy and recognition) when it comes to inspiring greater work performance. That said, as the late motivational speaker Zig Ziglar once remarked, "Money is not everything, but it ranks right up there with oxygen." The point is that while "money isn't everything," you should not be bashful about setting financial goals. Remember that you will ultimately be paid based on the value you offer to those whom you serve, meaning your employer and your customers. The monetary rewards from your career are tangible assets that you should manage through setting financial goals.

"Bucket List" goals. The final category of goals is very much an intrinsically driven category. What are some aspirations that you have that might be also described as dreams or wishes? These items could be prospects for your "bucket list" goals. This name, which derived its meaning as an extension of the common expression "kick the bucket" (meaning a list of things you wish to do before you die) gained great popularity in the aftermath of the 2007 Hollywood movie *The Bucket List* in which Jack Nicholson and Morgan Freeman portrayed two patients in a hospital cancer ward who escaped to pursue a wish list of things they want to do before they died. Maybe your situation is not as dire as it was for those two characters; but compiling a list of accomplishments, adventures, or experiences you wish to fulfill at some point in your life can intrinsically motivate you to pursue them and avoid having regrets like "what if.?" later in life.

So what exactly do bucket list goals look like? It is a list of what intrigues or interests you in some way. Examples may include:

- Going skydiving.
- Learning to speak French.
- Running a marathon in all 50 states.
- Attending a Super Bowl.
- Making peace with an old friend.

The list is yours to make; pursuit of bucket list goals adds a dimension of quality of life that cannot be experienced through the other goal categories.

Time Horizon

In addition to setting goals for different "life parts," you will also greatly benefit by breaking out and analyzing your goals across varying lengths of time.

The time frame you choose to organize your goals is up to you, but a widely used time horizon framework is to set short-range, mid-range, and long-range goals. Where goals fall in this classification scheme depends on the effort required or complexity to reach the outcome.

Short-range goals. These are outcomes you wish to achieve within a single year. Perhaps the best known form of short-range goals—the infamous New Year's Resolutions—are set around January 1 each year. Losing weight, saving money, raising your grade point average—all worthy accomplishments—are common examples of short-range goals that people set for a 12-month time frame each New Year's. It is estimated that about 40% of Americans make New Year's resolutions while only about 8% achieve them.[5] Not a ringing endorsement for setting short-range goals, is it?

One reason for the dismal success rate for New Year's resolutions is that the annual goal is not supported by setting incremental goals within an even shorter time horizon that if accomplished would speed a person toward completion of the annual goal. For example, if you set a financial goal of adding $1,000 to your savings account within 12 months, actually getting to that figure may seem impossible. What if you broke down that goal to $250 per quarter, or $83.33 per month, or $19.23 per week? Would that smaller goal seem more within reach? Of course it does! Breaking down one goal into shorter time periods of achievement is a helpful way to direct your actions on a daily, weekly, or monthly basis to ensure that you are progressing toward the desired outcome.

Mid-range goals. Although you can accomplish quite a bit in the span of 12 months, some goals you aspire to reach will take longer to achieve. Mid-range goals are those outcomes that can be more likely attained within one to three years. Earning a master's degree, completing a training program, or receiving a promotion are examples of personal growth that—while they must be worked on daily—require a longer time commitment to reach.

Mid-range goals work in concert with short-range goals as short-range goals establish benchmarks for progressing toward mid-range goals. The goal of earning a master's degree in two years could, for instance, be complemented with short-range goals of taking a minimum of two courses per semester, committing to 15 hours weekly on school-related activities, and/or setting aside one hour daily for reading.

Long-range goals. Ideally, you want to have some goals that are "big ideas" for what you can do or become over a longer period of time. Long-range goals have a time frame of three to five years, or perhaps even longer. Like mid-range goals, long-range goals require a broader time horizon to complete—even if you know now what you want to achieve.

If you have a goal of becoming a partner in a public accounting firm, realizing that goal is not an overnight proposition. Attaining partner status usually requires 10 years or more of experience in a firm. Of course, "doing time" is not a guaranteed gateway to advancement either; what you do to differentiate your brand and add value through your performance during those years is what really determines whether or not you will reach your long-range goal.

Again, it bears repeating that to ultimately make long-range goals a reality, you should commit to setting short-range and even mid-range goals that underwrite achievement of the long-range goal. A mix of short-range, mid-range, and long-range goals are needed to guide how you set priorities and spend your time. Keep in mind the saying that "the best way to eat an elephant is one bite at a time."

Reaching your goals is never easy; if it were, more people would set and achieve goals! But, if you commit to setting goals across these three time horizons, you help yourself immeasurably by matching actions with aspirations.

Use goals to "eat the elephant" and make seemingly difficult accomplishments easier to digest and achieve.

How to Set Goals

You are likely convinced that you need to join the small minority of people who set personal goals. You also probably have strong ideas about life parts and time horizon goals that you want to pursue. However, there is one more aspect of goals that you must understand before the power of goal setting can truly work for you and that is to fashion criteria for setting an effective goal. Do not be misled in to thinking that merely setting a goal puts you ahead of the pack that does not set goals. Your goals must be "SMART," an acronym that reminds us that goals should be:

- Specific
- Measurable
- Achievable
- Reaches
- and accomplished in a defined Time Frame.

Specific

A key role that goals play in personal growth is that they create accountability. If you state your intention to achieve something by setting a goal, you have made a personal commitment to making it happen (or at least making a hearty effort to achieve it).

In order for goals to have accountability, they must specifically state the outcome or result that is to occur. Otherwise, you do not know what exactly the end result should look like! So, for instance, if you decide to set a wellness goal to lose weight, you must set a specific weight or weight loss target to reach:

Not specific: "I will lose weight."

Specific: "I will lose 12 pounds."

A stark difference is observed between these two statements. The first one is not very helpful because it does not direct you to a clear outcome. You could lose one pound and meet the goal as written.

Another flaw in setting goals that are not specific is that they lack the personal accountability to which you need to be held. For instance, you could pat yourself on the back for losing three pounds if your goal is a vague "I will lose weight." However, if losing 12 pounds is what you really need to do to be in a more appropriate weight range (and enjoy the health benefits that come from it) then losing three pounds isn't sufficient to achieve your actual goal.

Finally, goals give direction for the actions and behaviors needed in the short run to get where you want to be in the long run. Goals that are specific can be broken down into daily and weekly checkpoints that advance you toward meeting your goal. A goal to lose 12 pounds in three months breaks down to just over 0.9 pounds per week.

Now, which target seems easier to hit? Twelve pounds? Or 0.9 pounds?

Measurable

When goals are written to be specific, they usually meet another criterion: the desired outcome must be measurable. In other words, you have to be able to determine if you reached a goal or how well you performed against the goal.

Going back to the weight loss example, making it specific (lose 12 pounds) also makes it measurable by having a quantifiable indicator— pounds as weighed by as scale. Performance against some goals is directly observable when it comes to weight loss, earning or saving a certain amount of money, or attending a set number of networking events.

Other goals do not lend themselves so easily to direct measurement. Thus, you need to ensure that indicators exist that could be used to evaluate performance. For example, you might desire to strengthen the quality of relationships with people with whom you are connected on LinkedIn. That goal is somewhat specific—you identified the network on which you will focus on building stronger relationships.

The problem is that a direct indicator does not exist. Overcome this problem by setting a measurable outcome *related* to the goal, such as "I will email five connections in my LinkedIn network each week to maintain and improve professional relationships." Now, here's a caveat. Be careful not to confuse activity with outcomes. While the activity of emailing connections can be measured, your goal is not to send emails. Your goal is to have better relationships with your connections.

Achievable

The underlying purpose for setting goals is to foster personal growth. But that growth cannot be realized if outcomes are not realistically attainable. Growth must be tempered with realism.

Setting a goal of earning $100,000 in the first year after you graduate college would be unrealistic if you were beginning your professional career in an entry-level retail management position where the median salary for retail manager trainee is about $37,000[6].

A greater concern with setting goals that are not achievable is that failure to reach them could have the unintended effect of demotivating you. If the bar is set too high and cannot be reached, you may give up and walk away from the bar rather than resetting it to a more achievable performance level.

One step you can take to minimize the possibility that your goals are too ambitious is to conduct a little research. If you are starting your career as a financial planner and want to set an income goal, consult industry data on what the average salary is for someone at your career stage. Don't want to settle for average and want to be in the top 10% of earners? That is great! Do the research to find out what top performers earn. Use that information as a frame of reference when setting your income goal.

Ensuring that goals are achievable is not intended to throw water on your ambitions. Rather, it is to help you set goals that can be reasonably met (and celebrated) instead of aiming for results you cannot possibly hit (which leaves you feeling defeated).

Reaches

The "reach" criterion might seem a bit contradictory after just being cautioned against setting goals that are too ambitious, but it is important that the outcomes set make you "stretch."

Building reach into goals is intended to move you out of your comfort zone, that place where you have some certainty about what outcomes you will get based on past experience. Professional development expert Brian Tracy says that comfort zones are among the greatest enemy of human potential.[7] The reason is that when we find our comfort zone, it is just that—comfortable.

So, why would we want to step away from comfort and into discomfort? We need to do so because it is necessary to first step out and reach before we can experience breakthrough achievement that advances our careers or other life parts requiring more than what our current performance or actions are producing.

A popular saying is that the definition of insanity is to repeat the same actions over and over and yet expect different results. Similarly, significant personal growth cannot be experienced by doing the same things you are currently doing and have always done. The challenge is to set targets that represent advancement from your current situation but at the same time that are within reach if you commit to the necessary actions. Reaching to achieve goals should lead to improvement, even if you do not fully hit a target that you set.

Time Frame

Create some certainty (and, in some instances, urgency) for your goals by stating the time frame in which you will achieve them.

A goal that meets the other criteria (specific, measurable, achievable, reaches) should not be set as an open-ended challenge. Put a deadline or target date for meeting the goal.

One of the benefits of setting time horizon goals is that they have a built-in time frame or realization period by virtue of being time-based outcomes in the first place. Putting a goal in a time frame also makes it more specific and therefore more real, tangible or reachable (or pressing!). Not only is the outcome itself observable, but a point in time in which it should be measured is established.

Time frame also relates to the Achievable and Reaches criteria in that you must be careful not to not set unrealistic time frames for accomplishments. At the same time, don't be so conservative that your goal does not push you to stretch your capabilities!

Let's return one last time to the goal of losing 12 pounds. Give this target a time period in which the weight loss or change should occur. The time frame should walk the line between being achievable and ever motivating you to reach to achieve. Don't set yourself up for failure with a goal like "I will lose 12 pounds by my wedding day, which is two weeks from today." Similarly, don't be too easy on yourself by saying "I will lose 12 pounds sometime over the next three years." Yes, you could probably meet that goal! However, the lack of urgency may not spark the motivation that could make it happen for you much sooner.

Take Action

Ask yourself these important questions before we proceed with the process of building your personal brand.

1. Have a "dream session" in which you create a list of what you would like to be, do, or have using the six life parts as categories:

   - Career
   - Relationships
   - Wellness
   - Spiritual
   - Financial
   - Bucket List

2. Select outcomes from your dream session list that you are willing to commit to pursuing. Write goals related to those outcomes using the SMART approach (the number of goals to set is up to you, but only set goals you are willing to take the necessary steps and actions to reach). Once you have them, begin to live them! Don't let your list get buried in a notebook or lost on a computer.

PART THREE: MAKEUP— BUILDING THE PRODUCT

8.

SKILL SET

"You better have some skills in this world. You better bring something to the dinner party, or you will be the dinner."
—Bryant McGill, author and activist

Skills = Product Development

Now that you have completed the process of defining personal brand Meaning, the next phase in personal brand building is to determine the ingredients needed to make the "product" you wish to become.

Some personal branding experts bristle at the idea of thinking of a person is a product. After all, you are a human being, not a pair of jeans! But too skeptical a view of "product" being part of personal branding overlooks a true constant in marketing: Products are what we market. Without a product designed to meet the needs of others, there is no need for activities commonly associated with marketing, such as advertising and other promotion tactics.

Accept it. Yes, you are a product, and the quality of that product will be decided by the investments you make in creating an offering that is valued by professors, employers, and clients alike – really, to anyone to whom you must "sell."

Makeup is the dimension of a personal brand that encompasses the skills, education, experience, and attitude needed to position yourself to compete in your chosen field. If you think about it, the Makeup of a personal brand, then, is much like the development of a product brand.

In the product development process, a combination of engineering and design considerations goes into producing a product that customers value, all supporting the mission of the organization (i.e., consistency with brand Meaning). Like a product brand, the significance of personal brand Makeup is not necessarily your attributes (such as the formal education you have completed or the specific skills you possess); instead, it is the substance.

Here's another way to look at it. You may be familiar with the idea that people do not buy product attributes, but rather that they buy benefits that the attributes deliver. Likewise, the value offered through your personal brand is not the courses you have taken or the knowledge you possess but rather is what you can do or produce through your Makeup attributes. That's substance.

Our exploration of Makeup begins with understanding a vital component of you as a product: your skills. Brand Meaning elements of purpose and passion are little more than dreams if you lack the skills needed to be a competent professional in your field.

Here's a key. The production of "Brand You" requires that you recognize the roles that two types of skills—hard skills and soft skills—play in creating the Makeup needed to compete. Then, comparing skills required against your strengths and weaknesses will help guide your decisions regarding the additional training and development you might need to position yourself for success.

Hard Skills

When you are taking stock of the skills required in a certain job or profession, it is likely that hard skills come to mind. Hard skills are those skills that can be taught, wherein understanding and ability can be demonstrated and performance can be measured. They are learned skills in which rules tend to stay the same regardless of company, circumstances, or the people you work with.

Hard skills can be learned through formal education or training.[1] Becoming a professional in fields such as accounting, chemistry, computer science, and engineering, for example, typically require completing a formal curriculum or program of study in order to earn a college degree. Demonstrating proficiency in hard skills often goes even beyond acquiring knowledge in a classroom and demands ongoing training and professional development throughout a career. For example, an aspiring financial securities sales professional must not only build foundational knowledge by taking finance and economics courses but also pass the Series 7 examination, a 250 question test administered by the Financial Industry Regulatory Authority (FINRA).[2]

Hard skills is an umbrella term covering a wide variety of different types of job-specific skills. For example, taking a look at hard skills associated with the information systems (IS) field can be broken out into three types: technical skills, programming skills, and business skills (see Figure 8.1). The mix of skills and number of different skills required varies by job or industry. For an early-career IS professional, it is likely that a premium would be placed on technical and programming skills. That's not to say that business skills are unimportant, as they are essential to understand how IS interacts with other departments in an organization. However, the depth of knowledge required might depend on the job's role. For example, a project manager would need to have stronger business skills than a SQL developer. The point is that as you prepare to turn professional in your chosen field, develop a list of needed skills across different hard skills types.

Technical Skills	Programming Skills	Business Skills
Software Development	SQL	Accounting
Information Management	.NET	Finance
Business Applications	AJAX	Marketing
Hardware	PHP	Supply Chain Management
	PERL	Project Management
	Java	Budgeting

Figure 8.1 Hard Skills Inventory for Information Systems Professional

Adapted from: Andrew Aken and Michael Michellsin (2007),"The Impact of the Skills Gap on the Recruitment of MIS Graduates," in *Proceedings of the 2007 ACM SIGMIS CPR conference on Computer personnel research: The global information technology workforce* (pp. 105-111), ACM.

Taking Inventory: What Hard Skills Do You Need?

It is impossible to list hard skills needed for career success in this space because there would be as many different lists as there are jobs! Each profession has a distinct set of hard skills, which are usually comprised of a blend of technical and business skills that are essential to perform competently.

More useful is to identify approaches to building a list of the hard skills you will need to acquire to strengthen your brand in a given field.

Recognizing the need for a list is the easy part; determining what the contents of that list should be is far more challenging. Consider these sources when gathering information about the hard skills required for your chosen field:

Job postings. A logical place to begin your exploration of needed hard skills for a given job you desire (now or in the future) is to search job postings online. A large number of postings across a wide range of fields can be found on career websites like Monster, CareerBuilder, and Glassdoor. Search filters on these websites allow you to tailor searches by industry, keywords relating to job title or position, and geographic area. If you have pinpointed an industry or field to which you aspire to work, you may find niche, career-related websites that enable you to focus your search exclusively within that industry. For example, if you want to work in sports business, a website like TeamWork Online will clearly be a more valuable resource for identifying hard skills sought by employers in that industry than the general classifieds section in the local paper. Job postings by organizations looking to fill positions generally scream out the teachable, technical skills that a candidate is expected to have in order to get an opportunity to work in that field.

One final note on job postings. Keep in mind that when a company posts an open job, the description of skills and traits desired represents the *perfect* candidate. Of course a company would want a new hire to at least possess, if not be strong in, every characteristic included in the job announcement. If you are not the perfect candidate, do not be discouraged… there may not be a single applicant that fits the description of the desired candidate 100%.

Social Networking Websites. A noteworthy characteristic of social networking sites is that they are a virtual gathering place around specific interests, including careers. Twitter and LinkedIn stand out as social networking sites that can be invaluable information resources on hard skills.

Use Twitter to create lists around your career interests. If your goal is to become a lawyer specializing in intellectual property (IP), you should use Twitter to follow professionals, companies, and organizations involved in that specific area of law practice. Similarly, an aspiring IP lawyer should utilize LinkedIn to follow lawyers and firms offering intellectual property services (and to identify possible future career opportunities that are better than their current circumstances). Also, use the LinkedIn Groups feature to join a community of professionals in your aspirational field. The benefit of employing these tactics is that you are able to follow what's going on in your field, including learning about developments in hard skills being sought by employers. (More about the career building benefits of Twitter and LinkedIn will be shared in chapters 13 and 14, respectively.)

Trade and Professional Organizations. It is not uncommon for organizations competing in the same industry to join forces to promote their interests by forming a trade or professional association. An important function of industry associations is often educational outreach or professional development.

The long-term health of any industry depends heavily on identifying and developing talented people who seek to obtain jobs in a given field. An example of an industry that makes the education of future professionals a priority is concrete management. The Concrete Industry Management National Steering Committee represents approximately ten different trade associations that represent the concrete industry. Its aim is to work with universities to develop concrete industry management professionals. The websites of those associations provide a vast amount of information on career paths and available jobs, skills sought in respective career pathways, and information on the hard skills taught by college degree programs.

Another purpose of such groups is to pool resources to promote their industry as a desirable career opportunity. Don't be reluctant to reach out personally in order to learn more about what hard skills you should develop as you prepare to turn professional. Remember that members of a trade or industry association were once in the position you may be at now, which is standing on the outside seeking to learn how to get in!

Practitioners. A more personal approach to gathering information about the hard skills needed to perform a particular job is to talk with someone who is already a professional in that field. Someone who does the job daily is uniquely positioned to inform you about the skill sets that you will need to possess to join that field or industry. You will find that many professionals are ready and willing to help as they see it as their way of "paying it forward" since they, too, likely sought and received guidance from established practitioners when they began their own career journey.

103

ME

The pool of potential contacts for discussing hard skills is larger today than ever thanks to the Internet. You can easily connect with professionals by using the social networking tools discussed previously. Do not overlook potential contacts from more traditional sources—relatives, family friends, or friends of friends, either. Whether you are making connections with practitioners digitally or face-to-face, all such contacts can be valuable information sources about the current hard skills you will be required to have right now, as well as predictions about new skills or competencies industry professionals will need in the future.

Teachers. One other traditional contact that can be a direct source of information on hard skills requirements are teachers. If you are a college student (or a former student who has maintained contact with some of your professors), tapping the wisdom of teachers can be beneficial in two ways. First, professors typically have professional contacts in the industry related to their field of expertise. They tend to stay up-to-date about the hard skills employers seek from new hires. Professors can be a connector to industry associations and practitioners you can reach out to for additional information. Next, many teachers and professors were practitioners prior to their teaching career. They have "been there, done that" and can personally give you a candid assessment of the skills that you need to build as you prepare to launch your career.

Strengthening Hard Skills

Once you have a good understanding of the essential hard skills required for success in your chosen field, the next step is to determine your options for acquiring or strengthening those hard skills needed to compete. Two paths that you can follow to get hard skills training is formal education and self-directed education.

Formal Education. The default option traditionally selected for acquiring needed hard skills is participation in formal education programs. Technical schools, community colleges, and colleges and universities are the institutions people look to for the training that will equip them with the hard skills needed to compete in a chosen field.

Two primary considerations when evaluating whether investing in formal education is the appropriate route for acquiring hard skills are the

104

specific skills enhanced through the curriculum and a cost/benefit analysis of attendance.

First, does the curriculum of a given academic program include training in the hard skills desired by employers? For example, if your career interest is working in social media marketing, does the program of study for the degree you would receive (e.g., marketing or public relations) include training in the specific tools of the trade such as a social media dashboard like Hootsuite and a blogging platform like WordPress?

Another consideration for a degree program is whether internships are encouraged or even required. Many benefits can be realized from doing an internship, but one in particular related to hard skills is that if the curriculum for a major does not include on-site exposure to a particular hard skill (e.g., software for managing social media accounts), experience can be obtained through an internship experience that adds to your hard skills set.

A second consideration about whether to pursue formal education to acquire needed hard skills is a comparison of costs to acquire versus benefits received. Perhaps the worst kept secret in America is that the cost to attend college has risen steadily for many years. In comparison to costs for other personal expenses, the cost of higher education has run away over the past three decades. Since 1978, the cost of tuition and fees have skyrocketed 1,225%.[3]

While the rising cost of higher education and burden of student loan debt that many students take on cannot be ignored, the cost of acquiring a formal education must be weighed against benefits of building your hard skills set. A Pew Research study of Millennials aged 25-32 found the average earnings of someone with a four-year college degree to be about $45,000, compared to $30,000 for persons with a two-year degree or some college (and $28,000 with no formal education beyond high school).[4] It is important to note that while earning a four-year degree is by no means a magical remedy for career woes, statistics point out a direct relationship between making a commitment to building hard skills through formal education and employment stability compared to others who do not pursue a formal, four-year college experience.

A formal education alternative to a two-year or four-year college degree is a certificate program. Colleges and universities offer certificates in rather specialized fields of study in contrast to the more diverse subject curriculum of a traditional bachelor's degree. The focused curriculum means that a certificate program can usually be completed in a matter of months.

For example, George Mason University in Virginia offers a certificate in Human Resource Management. The program focuses on training in specialized areas of the field, including compensation and benefits, employee and labor relations, and risk management.[5] A certificate program may be ideal for professionals who have already earned a college degree already and are seeking to position themselves for a higher position in their field (or to earn the certificate to acquire the additional hard skills needed to make a career change to a new field).

Ultimately, no matter what path you choose to achieve them, you must parlay your hard skills into a distinctive personal brand that enhances your marketability.

Self-Directed Education. Formal education received in pursuit of a degree or certificate can provide the needed credentials to "make the cut," or achieve the minimum requirements an employer finds essential in order to be considered for a job. However, the cost of obtaining a formal education can be financially crippling for many students. One study on student loan indebtedness found that the Class of 2014 had the dubious distinction of being the most indebted class ever, owing an average of $33,000 in student loans.[6]

For many professions, formal education may be the only option to enter your chosen field. But, if a degree or certificate obtained from formal education is not mandatory, self-directed education could be a far less expensive alternative to gain hard skills sought.

Many options exist for a do-it-yourself approach to building hard skills, with the most popular ones being free online courses, skill-specific training, and public online resources. Free online courses today are packaged in what are known as massive open online courses, referred to in shorthand as MOOCs. These courses are offered by more than 100 universities across America, including prestigious institutions such as Harvard, Stanford, and Vanderbilt. Although MOOCs have been in existence only since the late 2000s, the number of participants enrolled in courses has grown dramatically. The largest MOOC organization, Coursera, offers nearly 800 different courses to its approximately 10 million users. Subjects range from traditional academic disciplines like calculus and chemistry to emerging topics including environmental sustainability and mobile cloud computing.[7] Users have the option of taking courses for free and strictly for personal development or to pay to receive a certificate as proof of completion. Time frames in which courses are offered vary, typically lasting five to 12 weeks and occurring throughout the year. MOOCs are a low-risk option for determining if you have the aptitude to build hard skills needed for a particular job or field.

A second way to acquire specific hard skills without going through formal programs such as those offered at a college or university is to take skill-specific courses online. While it is possible that you might find YouTube videos that are helpful in learning a particular skill, you will probably benefit more from seeking out training that is professionally planned and produced.

Two sources of skill-specific learning platforms are Udemy and Lynda. Udemy offers more than 20,000 courses teaching skills in areas such as Java programming language, digital photography, and Portuguese. Some courses are free but most have fees ranging from $9 to $499. Learners can complete courses at their own pace. Lynda positions itself slightly differently, calling itself a platform for online tutorials. Training tends to be rather specific; examples include video editing, designing an e-book, and analyzing data using Microsoft Excel. Lynda users pay a monthly membership fee that gives them unlimited access to the more than 128,000 videos in its library.[8]

A third broad category of self-directed learning materials is the vast amount of free video and blogs on the Internet. Perhaps the best known video platform for personal development is TED Talks. This collection consists of more than 1,800 videos from the internationally known TED (Technology, Entertainment, and Design) conferences. TED speakers are generally known as leaders in their respective fields. Although the format of TED Talks bears little resemblance to the formal learning platforms discussed previously in this section, they nevertheless impact viewers by exposing them to cutting-edge thinking that allows learners to "sit at the feet" of some of the world's brightest people.

Blogs should be another consideration in any self-directed education program. Blogs maintained by companies and experts in their chosen fields should be regular reading for someone trying to enter those fields, and part of a routine daily or weekly discipline of how an individual spends time online. I (Don) have a number of blogs grouped in the online reader (Feedly) under a category called "Must Read Blogs." These blogs are from various thought leaders in marketing, including Seth Godin, Chris Brogan, Mark Schaefer, and Mitch Joel. Other blogs followed are in fields related to jobs and interests (including higher education, marketing, sports business, and social media). Blogs are an extremely useful source of information to keep abreast with what is going on in a particular field, including the hard skills required to succeed within that field.

You have many options for acquiring and developing hard skills. Regardless of how you do it, keep this in mind: 60% of new jobs require skills that only 20% of workers currently have.[9] Sharpening hard skills is a never-ending project.

Soft Skills

Hard skills are essential in every profession. Certain technical knowledge and abilities specific to performing a task or role must be possessed in order to be a viable job candidate. But hard skills are not enough.

Does that statement surprise you? Do you believe that if you have the hard skills required to perform a job, you are sure to meet employer expectations? Well, you're not. You must develop another set of capabilities for your skills "toolbox" that complements your "how to" skills with a more intangible set.

This second set of skills is known as soft skills. In a nutshell, they are management and people skills. Unlike hard skills, soft skills are difficult to teach in formal learning environments, and the mastery of soft skills is more difficult to measure compared to hard skills.[10]

Don't be fooled by the label "soft." Given that label, it could be tempting to interpret that these skills are somehow less important or impactful to your professional development. Quite by contrast, one study found that 77% of employers believe soft skills are just as important as hard skills when evaluating job candidates. Specifically, work ethic, dependability, and positive attitude were the soft skills valued most in prospective employees.[11]

Let's dig deeper into soft skills and how they impact your personal brand Makeup.

Why Soft Skills Matter

In many professions, career preparation focuses on math, science, or technical skills required for performance (hard skills). However, our ever-changing business environment now calls for complementing technical training with the development of soft skills.

Evidence of negative consequences stemming from not possessing strong soft skills is found to be particularly acute in the field of information technology, one in which professionals get jobs and advance presumably through accumulating breadth or depth in technical knowledge, defined as different programming languages "spoken" or grasp of emerging technologies. However, a survey of technical professionals found that 40 to 70% of projects end in failure (i.e., are not completed or completed over budget or past deadline). Why? The number one reason cited was lack of soft skills. Face-to-face communication, nonverbal communication, active listening, writing, and presentation skills were all found to be important soft skills for technical professionals to develop (and that many are presently lacking).[12]

Soft skills require emotional intelligence, which is also known as EQ. According to a top researcher into emotional intelligence, Daniel Goleman, EQ includes self-awareness, self-regulation, motivation, empathy, and social skills.[13] Emotional intelligence refers to a person's ability to identify, assess, and control the emotions of self, of other individuals, and of groups. Emotional intelligence consists of two types of traits: a personal component (stress management, self-awareness, and perseverance), as well as traits that deal with social competencies (meeting, teamwork, negotiation, selling, and interviewing).[14]

Daniel Goleman calls emotional intelligence "a different way of being smart." The good news is that you can raise your EQ to develop a broader, more complete array of soft skills. You must first know the current state of your soft skills development.

What Soft Skills Do You Need?

So what exactly are these soft skills that are so important to your Makeup?

Career success expert Lei Han groups 28 different soft skills into two categories: self-management skills and people skills. Both soft skill types share certain characteristics, including not having clear cut, "black and white" rules for acquiring skills, being portable from one position to another or one organization to another, and being mastered by embarking on a journey of skill development and refinement.[15]

Self-management skills. A collection of self-management skills is listed in Figure 8.2. These soft skills are essential to developing an inner strength and confidence that will contribute to your career success.

Soft Skill	Description
Growth mindset	Commit to learning and self-improvement
Self-awareness	Know what inspires, drives, and angers you
Emotion regulation	Manage emotions to make objective decisions
Self-confidence	Believe in yourself and ability to do anything
Stress management	Stay calm and balanced in different situations
Resilience	Bounce back after set back and move on
Forgive and forget	Get over wrongs- yours and others
Perseverance	Maintain energy and dedication to achieve
Patience	Step back and think clearly
Perceptiveness	Interpret and analyze actions to understand

Figure 8.2 Self-Management Skills

Adapted from: Lei Han (2014, n.d.). Soft Skills List- 28 Skills to Working Smart. Retrieved from https://bemycareercoach.com/soft-skills/list-soft-skills.html.

Skills such as a growth mindset, self-confidence, and persistence can build momentum through greater awareness of your capabilities and position you for advancement opportunities. Acquiring self-management skills like stress management, emotion regulation, and persistence serve to protect you against adversity, disappointments, "moving on" after making mistakes, and overcoming failure.

This subset of soft skills enhances your emotional preparedness. Before you can add value for others (e.g., clients or fellow employees) through your professional role, you must first have your own house in order. Reflect on the self-management skills in Figure 8.2 to assess which skills could be the most advantageous to you and also which ones represent areas of improvement needed to build your soft skills set.

People Skills. You have likely heard the term "people skills" from teachers, parents, or bosses. It refers to a person's abilities to interact with or manage other people. The absence of people skills can lead a hiring manager or supervisor to conclude that someone is not a desirable employee because he or she is not a "people person" even though they might have well-developed hard skills. People skills are needed to effectively interact with others, including your peers, your boss, clients, and others, as well as to exert influence over others if you assume a leadership role. Figure 8.3 lists 18 people skills (which are also soft skills) that are relevant to your brand Makeup.

It is generally agreed upon that people skills are important; the challenge you face is learning the expectations of employers for the soft skills desired and needed to position you for success.

For example, what exactly does it mean to have good communication skills (how is it defined, measured, or observed)? The same point can be made for the other 17 people skills listed in Figure 8.3. Are they important? The answer is a resounding "yes." But how you define, learn, and measure these skills vary across organizations and managers.

Building Soft Skills

You may have heard the difference between hard skills and soft skills referred to as "book sense" versus "common sense." While it is true that hard skills are learned through some means of instruction such as "book learning," you should not rely on common sense alone for strengthening soft skills.

The same methods for learning hard skills discussed earlier in this chapter are applicable for soft skill development, too. For example, persuading others in negotiation situations is a valuable soft skill whether you are a business school student or an established sales professional. You could

Conventional	Tribal
(Found in most job descriptions)	(Gained from experience, mentors)
– Communication	– Managing upward
– Teamwork	– Self-promotion
– Interpersonal relationships	– Dealing with difficult personalities
– Presentation	– Dealing with unexpected situations
– Meeting management	– Handling office politics
– Facilitating	– Influence/persuasion
– Selling	– Negotiation
– Managing	– Networking
– Leadership	
– Mentoring	

Figure 8.3 People Skills
Adapted from: Lei Han (2014, n.d.). Soft Skills List- 28 Skills to Working Smart.
Retrieved from https://bemycareercoach.com/soft-skills/list-soft-skills.html.

fulfill your need to strengthen negotiation skills by pursuing the following options:

Formal education. Colleges and universities of all sizes ranging from the Harvard Negotiation Institute and Stanford University to local institutions offer negotiation courses and certificate programs.

Self-Directed Education. Becoming more proficient at negotiation does not require you enroll in a higher education course or program. Coursera offers a free course from the University of Michigan called Successful Negotiation: Essential Strategies and Skills. Udemy offers the course "Problems Solved, Not Battles Fought." Even more informal approaches to sharpening negotiation skills include reading books written by experts on the topic, such as the classic *Getting to Yes* by Roger Fisher, William Ury, and Bruce Patton. Blogs, audio books, and podcasts are other sources of self-directed learning that could be used to expand your knowledge of negotiation.

Striving to improve in other soft skills can be pursued in the same manner as it is outlined here for negotiation. The learning resources are out there; you simply must decide which ones fit your learning style best and then go to work improving yourself. Regardless of the resources used, the point is to take advantage of them to work on the development of the soft skills needed to make you more valuable to employers as you prepare to "turn pro" (or to become a better pro).

Being competent in hard skills needed in your chosen profession is no longer sufficient for career success. Soft skills equip you to thrive in organizational environments that are becoming less bureaucratic and more social.

Hard skills and soft skills are vital pieces in your personal brand Makeup. Consider the following statistics if you are still not convinced about the importance of skills development:

- *Hard skills get you in the door*—69% of human resources professionals say that they look first at an applicant's hard skills to determine if they are viable candidates.
- *Soft skills get you the job*—56% of human resources professionals say the most important abilities in new hires are soft skills, especially interpersonal relations.[16]

Take Action

Skill set is the very core of personal brand Makeup. Even a clearly defined Meaning and consistent Message cannot compensate for deficiencies in brand Makeup caused by insufficient skill development. Ask yourself these important questions before we proceed with the process of building your personal brand.

1. Identify the hard skills that a professional in the field you have chosen or are considering pursuing possesses by tapping information sources mentioned in this chapter (job postings, social networking websites, trade/professional organizations, practitioners, and teachers). Which skills do you possess already?

   Is the lack of a particular hard skill (or skills) preventing you from landing the job that you want? If yes, what is the more realistic option for gaining needed skills—formal education, self-directed education, or both?

2. Refer to the self-management and people skills lists in Figures 8.2 and 8.3. For each of these soft skills types, identify your three greatest strengths and your three greatest weaknesses. If possible, have someone who knows you well (e.g., a boss, friend, or mentor) rate your top strengths and weaknesses in the two soft skills types, too.

Skill Set

Don't rely on common sense alone to understand and strengthen your soft skills. Knowing the importance of soft skills and how to strengthen them is crucial to your career success. You've been working on your hard skills for years. Now it's time to understand and develop your soft skills – your people skills. In today's business environment, you must complement hard skills with soft skills. They're essential to developing the inner strength and confidence that will contribute to your career success.

What's Included in This Package

An analysis and development plan for your interpersonal and people oriented skills. These reports will help you understand how you interact with others and provide a roadmap to strengthen your people skills.

Take Action: Self-Assess NOW **http://bit.ly/SelfAssessME**

9.

MINDSET

"We like to think of our champions and idols as superheroes who were born different from us. We don't like to think of them as relatively ordinary people who made themselves extraordinary."

—Carol S. Dweck

Mindset Matters

Is developing the right mindset the key to unlocking the potential inside of each of us? Is mindset an important part of personal branding and something we should spend time understanding and developing as part of our personal brand? The unequivocal answer to both questions is yes.

In her book *Mindset*, Stanford University psychology professor Carol Dweck explained that there are two kind of mindsets. The first, a "fixed" mindset, is where a person accepts their level of intelligence or talent as who they are. As a result, they view success as something that is only for the strong or talented and do not see the benefit of trying to "grow" or change their own mindset.

The second, or what Dweck called a "growth" mindset, is characterized by how someone responds to adversity and how they view learning as the key indicators (or trail of bread crumbs) to finding the success they desire.

That analysis begs the question: Can we grow through struggle to ultimately find our success? Or, does innate talent predetermine how successful we can be?

While innate talent is something every individual possessing it should definitely tap into, understanding how we routinely respond to challenges as they are presented to us is equally important. It's those series of struggles that ultimately help define who we are, what we do, and why we matter. That's because it is in struggle that we change our mindset so that we can think better, communicate better, and make better decisions.

Cultivate a Growth Mindset

If you want more, you have to become more. There are many versions of this old saying, and seemingly ever more reasons in modern life that it still holds true today.

Becoming more, or growing, begins with expanding your mindset. Mindset is a complex element that colors the human experience like nothing else can or does. It is at the core of how you can create a bigger future for yourself because it is the very foundation for what you see, how you see it, and what you believe (or don't believe) can be done about it.

As humans, we all have the unique ability to make decisions and choose how we respond in almost every aspect of our life. Viktor Frankl, psychiatrist and Holocaust survivor, once stated that "Between stimulus and response, there is a space. In that space lies our freedom and power to choose our response. In our response lies our growth and freedom."

That space is our mindset, and it is the key to unlocking our own lifestyle, freedom, and (ultimately) opportunity.

A person's mindset is built over many years and from defining moments in a person's life that become the very makeup or substance of that person. Manu Bennett, an actor who played Crixus in the miniseries *Spartacus*, once said, "Anyone can train to be a gladiator. What marks you out is having the mindset of a champion." Making a decision to become a champion is at the core of cultivating a right mindset… whether you recognize it or not.

If your mindset is expanding along with your skill set, networks, and your ability to tell a story, then your personal brand is growing as well. Having a positive, strong growth mindset is the driving force that is the foundation for building a complete personal brand.

Within a growth mindset, people believe that their basic abilities can be developed through dedication, hard work, being intentional, and that their innate talent is simply a starting point for greatness. This view creates a self-directed, lifelong learner who is resilient, meaning they are not crushed by the first thing that goes wrong on any given day.

Developing a growth mindset creates motivation and productivity in both business and life relationships. A growth mindset allows a person to focus and clearly communicate with themselves and others about the value they offer. Last, cultivating a growth mindset allows a person to recognize and seize flashing moments of opportunity and make the most of them. If business is about communication and relationships, having a growth mindset allows you to recognize "flashing moments of opportunity" which can turn that moment from opportunity to productivity – in other words not just interviewing for the position, but. securing the position. Knowing your value and communicating it in that moment will be the difference between "growing" or staying where you currently are.

A Process Driven by Mindset

Nick Saban, the head football coach at The University of Alabama, has a system for developing individual and team potential called "The Process." It has been referred to as a philosophy, a way of life, and a mindset. Its purpose is to give his teams a competitive advantage by not focusing so much on the competition, but rather by looking within themselves and playing every play like it has a life of its own.

This approach changes the way Saban's players look at the game. A growing, positive mindset like the one this system fosters allows a person to challenge the status quo and think differently about the world around them. One of the core beliefs of this system is that those who understand the proper mindset possess a competitive advantage and despite occasional struggles can win.

In his blog, SportsonEarth.com, Lars Anderson wrote about Saban and the culture he creates with his football teams. He stated, "It was the fall of 1998 and he was in his fourth season at Michigan State. The Spartans were 4-4, and, in few days, were slated to travel to Columbus, Ohio to play undefeated Ohio State, the top ranked team in the nation.

Recalling the lessons of his father, Saban opted to try something new in practice that week. He told his players not to worry about winning the game. Rather, he instructed them to treat each play as if it was a game and to focus only on what needed to be done during that play to be successful. And as soon as the whistle blew on each play, it was to be wiped from memory; all that mattered was the next play and zeroing in on what actions needed to be completed in order to 'win' that play. Saban found during the week that his players appeared more confident and were as crisp in practice as they'd been all season. A 24-point underdog, Michigan State then went

119

into Columbus and upset the Buckeyes 28-24. A new element of The Process was born."

So how does this idea of a developing a "process" relate to you?

Education and Mindset

Let's look at the concept of mindset through the lens of one of the typical areas we generally focus on to determine success—education. Ask people why they achieved some level of education and they will usually tell you one of four reasons. The most popular reason people choose to further their education is their parents told them to do it. They may also say their friends are going to school so they chose to go as well. Another group will tell you it's how to become successful in a chosen career path. The last group will tell you they didn't have anything else to do and were eligible for student loans.

You must first be clear about why you want to pursue more education. In a growth mindset, additional schooling is viewed as a method or pathway to developing a bigger future. The focus is not on making the grade, but on learning the material and using it as a building block to success.

Ask yourself: is the focus for you on making the grade? Or on learning the material? If the focus is on making the grade, you may want to ask yourself why the grade is so important to you, or what you are really are trying to accomplish. If it's just to make a grade, then study the material and make the grade. If instead it is to learn, your focus may need to be redirected to how you can apply the information to create the future you want for yourself. These are two completely different mindsets with two entirely different outcomes. One is fixed while the other is inspired by growth.

As you ask these questions, take a look at some of the facts about those who chose to advance their careers through higher education:

- According to the U.S. Department of Education and American College Testing, 51% of college students at four-year colleges will transfer or dropout.
- Of this 51%, 30% transfer to another college or change their major, 20% transfer more than once and take more than six years

to finish, and 50% dropout completely.

- The College Board 2006-2007 Annual Survey of Colleges reports that the cost of each additional year in college at a four-year public in-state institution is $16,357.
- In the 2008 Graduating Senior Survey, when asked about immediate employment plans, 16% replied that they had "no idea."
- According to the National Association of Colleges and Employers (NACE) *2008 Job Outlook*, perhaps no attribute is more valued than experience. Approximately 95% of those responding factored in candidate experience when making hiring decisions (76.2% preferred relevant work experience while 18.2% preferred any type of experience).
- In a recent longitudinal study by the Bureau of Labor Statistics, individuals held an average of 10.8 jobs between the ages of 18 to 42, with the majority of the jobs being held before age 27.

These statistics paint a stark picture that clearly illustrates that a degree from an institution of higher learning will only go so far. Those who choose to pursue formal education must have a growth mindset with an intent to learn if they truly wish to take advantage of the opportunities college coursework presents.

Believe, Become, Act

Believing in yourself may be one of the most important elements in having the mindset needed to win in a competitive marketplace. Not believing in yourself will lead instead to low confidence and eventually low self-esteem. If you do not believe in yourself, most likely you have negative thoughts that will lead you to negative actions.

A positive mindset is crucial to becoming a successful entrepreneur, start a new business, or develop a new career path. Each one of these endeavors requires a proper and healthy mindset to deal with the risks that inevitably come along with such ventures. Accept and approve of yourself! Do not criticize your current life. Have unstoppable confidence and develop a "growing" mindset. Then, take action!

Still have doubts about the importance of believing, becoming, and taking action? According to America's Career Research Network

Association, statistics show that students with a career plan in mind while they are enrolled in college graduate on time and have higher academic success rates. After graduation, students who had a career plan in place secure better entry jobs, earn higher incomes, and experience less career change (and faster career advancement) than their contemporaries without a plan.

Having a positive attitude can lead to happiness, success, and effectively change your life. Attitude not only affects you but it can affect your environment and the people around you as well. It bolsters belief in your abilities and expertise, can motivate you to do great things in your day and in your life, and can motivate others as well.

The opposite is true of a negative attitude. Having a bad attitude leads to failure, to constantly focusing on why things are not working out the way you want them to work out, and has a deleterious impact on the people around you as well.

Mindset and Success

Mindset defines the way you think, how you feel, and what you do. Those who are intentional about the success they want to create are driven by a hunger to learn and grow. They understand that mindset can provide limitless opportunities, whereas not developing or focusing on mindset can hold you hostage.

Can a hardworking, driven person who believes in developing themselves regardless of how much raw talent they possess accomplish anything as long as they create a focus for their life and strive every day to achieve that? Those that subscribe to a growth mindset indeed can. A person with that same talent but a lack of drive and mental toughness will by comparison not reach those same heights of success.

Mindset is like a collection of keys on a key ring. There are many keys and many doors to choose from, but if you have the right key, and find the right door, it will in fact open for you. Of course, if you view mindset as a competitive advantage, you might also simply opt to kick the door down!

Isn't that what you want? Researchers Laura Kray and Michael Hasselhuhn found that business school students who were taught a growth mindset learned more skills and received better grades than their peers without it. Then at the professional level, when managers are taught a growth mindset, they are in turn more willing to coach their employees up, and the quality of their developmental coaching is better. Finally, leaders with the correct mindset want to learn how to improve their management techniques and are not threatened by the idea of hearing negative things about their leadership style. Regardless of professional status or position, mindset is the key to progress and success.

Mindset Travels with You

If a person develops the correct mindset, it goes with them throughout life. It doesn't matter where a person is or what new task they take on (or is thrust upon them). The mindset becomes a part of that person and walks hand and hand with them through every experience in life.

A strong mindset is the reason why successful people are asked over and over by random other professionals how they think and what they believe. A strong mindset is palpable and attracts that kind of attention and questioning. No wonder a correct mindset can work effectively and produce results across many different lines of work.

Take Action

The process of defining who you are begins with a personal assessment of your strengths and weaknesses. Consider your behavioral characteristics (mindset), the skills that you possess, and the expertise that you can demonstrate.

Acknowledging how you communicate, how you behave as a team member, what type of leadership competence you exhibit, and what contributions you typically make during meetings or social activities are essential components of this process. All of these attributes and skills will influence how you are defined.

1. You are also defined based on the value you contribute to others. Can you articulate your personal value proposition and is it consistent with how those around you recognize your value contribution? A hard look in the mirror to confront these questions can be a difficult task, but it is one that is essential to the personal branding process.

Questions that you should be asking that are related to mindset include:

- How are you different?
- How do you add value?
- Describe your typical communication behavior.
- Why should anyone listen to you?
- What are your life goals and do you have a plan?
- How are you reinventing yourself?
- How are you improving your skills?
- What steps are you taking to strategically position yourself as a prominent brand?
- How do others define who you are (parents, siblings, spouse, friends, colleagues, supervisors, and vendors)?
- Are you on "career cruise control" or are you committed to personal and professional growth?

2. Once you have reflected on these questions and answered them, review your responses to determine if they are consistent with a growth mindset or fixed mindset. If responses to any questions sound like they come from someone with a fixed mindset, consider how changing beliefs could alter your mindset. What needs to change in your thinking?

Mindset

"Mindset is like a collection of keys on a key ring. There are many keys and many doors to choose from, but if you have the right key, and find the right door, it will in fact open for you." Gain the confidence you need to focus and clearly communicate with yourself and others about the value that you offer.

What's Included in This Package

An interactive online tool that allows you to see more than 650 careers ranked in order according to your likes and dislikes. You'll be able to sort the careers by education levels, search for enjoyment levels related to specific careers or explore what you'd like or dislike about specific careers. You'll also have access to understanding your greatest strengths and your career development path based on your preferences, interests and motivations.

Take Action: Self-Assess NOW **http://bit.ly/SelfAssessME**

10.

CREATING AND ACTIVATING AN ATTRACTIVE NETWORK

"Networking is marketing. Marketing yourself, marketing your uniqueness, and marketing what you stand for."
—Christine Comaford-Lynch, entrepreneur and author

Creating a network in a professional sense can be one of the most difficult yet rewarding self-investments a person can make.

An often repeated saying related to networking is you are the sum total of the five people you spend the most time with. Step back and analyze who makes up your sum total. If those five people aren't compelling, or who you want to become, you need to quickly make some changes to re-fashion a network for yourself that will assist you in developing the connections you to need to find the success you desire (not keep you from it).

Networking, the verb, is the act of creating a network. And as seen from the opening quote in this chapter, networking is a marketing activity.

To get started, it's important to establish what a network is. Public research university Royal Holloway has defined networks as clusters of people who have common interests who are able to share knowledge in order to help one another in some way. There are many ways in which a network can be established.

The majority of people have some sort of network without even realizing it or utilizing it! One of the easier branches of a networking tree to grab ahold of is made up of those people you are surrounded by right now. If you are in college, that would likely be classmates, individuals you are in organizations with, professors, advisors, and possibly the people you meet in an internship.

In many cases, networks may already be established and you need to simply tap into them. For instance, for those graduating college soon (or who have done so recently), most universities have alumni associations that can provide a great jumpstart to your network.

Be Strategic

It is important to be strategic when connecting with people to add to your network. A good network consists of people willing to exchange advice, concerns, information, and, importantly, who are willing to refer you to other people.

People who are "in the know" are great people to have in your network. In doing so, they will be able to tell you about potential jobs, introduce you to their own contacts, and perhaps even get personally interested in hiring you—whether it be now or in the future.

As you grow in your career, so should (and do) the contacts in your network. That's in part because jobs change and industries change. Typically, as a result of all that, people in networks become more experienced, more knowledgeable, and more connected.

Activating your network and personal branding are directly tied to one another. Networking is essential to developing and maintaining your personal brand. In order to achieve professional goals, you must not only establish a network but create one that is extensive. Even if someone cannot assist you at the present moment, you never know who may help further your career in the future. The more people you network with, the more exposure you get for your brand. Hence, the larger your network is, the more value you bring to potential employers.

However, while establishing a network is key, it is useless unless you do know how to *use* your network.

Common Misconceptions

Now that you know what a network is, let's talk about what it isn't. When people build a network, especially twenty-something's that are on or will soon be on the job hunt, they sometimes confuse it with simply compiling a laundry list of names to whom they can hand their résumé. Here's a fact of human nature: Unless a person knows you, your résumé will likely get put in a pile somewhere and never be seen again.

Networking is also not the equivalent of asking for a job. People like to feel appreciated and valued. While you very well may be connecting with them because you have reason to believe that they can help you on your career path, blatantly asking them for your "dream job" probably isn't going to work.

Networking is about starting a relationship, feeding a relationship, and letting it simmer for the right time and place to take action when needed. Treated otherwise, your network is likely to feel "used" by you more than anything else.

Going to networking mixers are a great starting point to meet some initial contacts and gather business cards. But a stack of business cards will not help you much, either, unless you know how to use them. A business card is meant to serve as a vehicle by which you achieve or provide direct contact information. If you're not using the information you have but rather are simply collecting business cards, how helpful is that? Turn those business cards to actual contacts on your network and start heating up that relationship!

As with conducting a business deal, you should always be up-front about what you are seeking. Now, not so up-front that you say, "I want a job" even if that is indeed the case! Be up-front, rather, in the sense of giving people a clear sense of what you want to do, where you want to be, and how you think they may be able to help you (and, if applicable, how you can help them). If this isn't established, you could be putting a lot of time and energy into trying to create a lasting connection with someone who turns out to be completely unhelpful to you in your ongoing pursuit of career improvement.

Be Intentional About the Network You Create

Creating a network is not stalking executives or hiring managers with countless emails, phone calls, or LinkedIn notifications, either. Top managers of Fortune 500 companies are not going to respond to your queries (unless you give them a compelling reason to connect with you). Be reasonable with regards to who you reach out to and be sensible in how you connect with them.

Consider the following three assets outlined by researchers Brian Uzzi and Shannon Dunlap in the *Harvard Business Review* and consider how they could be invaluable to someone wanting to expand their network (or even if someone simply extends an invitation to you). "Networks deliver three unique advantages: private information, access to diverse skill sets, and power. Executives see these advantages at work every day, but might not pause to consider how their networks regulate them."

A lot of jobs are filled even before they are posted on a job board or become public knowledge. So how do these jobs get filled? Networking, plain and simple. If you are in the market for a new job, networking is the direct path to learning about new opportunities long before hundreds of resumes are submitted. When you are connected with those people with hiring power and you have fostered an intentional relationship with them, they will remember you at just the right time.

Taking a Traditional Approach

From your family to your friends to former co-workers, you can establish yourself as a candidate for opportunities by getting in touch with your personal network.

People don't know that you are looking for an opportunity if you don't tell them! Stay in touch with your contacts and offer assistance to them as well. There may not be an opening at the moment, but surely they will think of your name in the future when they become aware of an opportunity.

This is why you never want to burn bridges with your contacts. If someone can't help you at the moment, that doesn't mean they won't know someone who can or that they still won't be helpful to you in the future.

There is a fine line, however, between staying connected and looking desperate. Make personal phone calls, send letters, and ask your contacts out for coffee. Never point blank ask if they can get you a job. Instead, ask to shadow them for a day, or ask for advice on how you can break into an industry.

Last, making connections on social media is essential. Once you do, stay current with what you are posting and always keep your career objectives updated. You never know who can or might help! We will get into how to use social media for networking in Chapters 13 and 14.

Get On the List

Being recognized for your work in the community and in an industry can do wonders for activating your network.

Award ceremonies are helpful for building and activating networks and can even lead to business opportunities. Attend them and look to meet interesting people that add value to the community in unique ways.

Publications like those published by local business journals are usually very active with regards to activating their network and offering opportunities to learn about and recognize leaders in a particular field. Piggybacking on those publications, listservs and publication-sponsored events are other great ways to activate your network in a competitive landscape.

In 2010, when I (Colby) was selected a *Nashville Business Journal* "40 under 40" award recipient, my network grew exponentially almost overnight. The minute that list was released, my phone began to ring and my name became much better known in Nashville professional circles. In 2015, after accepting the Nashville Chamber of Commerce Impact Award, my network grew again. Once again my phone began to ring off the hook. If you can stand out among a sea of applicants by being recognized for your work, whether paid or unpaid, you will gain tremendous credibility among executives and recruiters alike.

Connecting at Conferences

Conferences can also be a strategic place to activate your network (or, alternately, to do like others do and sit on your phone while people walk by…not!) What better place to meet people to help fast forward your career trajectory than a gathering of professionals in your field?

Conferences provide individuals with the opportunity to get away from the deadline-driven, dog-eat-dog work environment and meet similar professionals in a more casual setting. Conferences also provide situations such as workshops, team building exercises, and social gatherings like dinners that provide almost limitless opportunities to share stories (specifically *your* story), ask for advice, and collaborate with other professionals. Conferences are also the best place to get referrals, obtain new contacts, make new friends, and come away with new opportunities and potential projects.

In a conference setting, you might only have two minutes to talk to a specific person, so be mindful of their time and be ready with the short version of your story.[1] Conference presenters in particular have a lot of people lined up for their time, so if you do not get the face time with them that you desire, just ask for their card or contact info and get in touch at a later date with a message referencing specifics about their speech. Do your best to then stay in touch with that person. Research the topic they spoke about so you have some background info on it, and highlight comments from their talk. Use their talk as an "in" to a bigger networking opportunity. Don't use what is called a 'cold email' where you basically just ask them to help you without either offering to reciprocate or even referencing elements of their speech that you enjoyed or that served you well. Failing to do so sounds like your sole purpose for reaching out to them is to get something from them.

Chances are if they are good enough to be a conference speaker, they have valuable experiences and vast networks themselves that you would be lucky to tap into. Connecting with speakers is a bit of an art form, but it can be a valuable tool in activating and advancing your networks.

Who Knows You?

Who knows you? It's a legitimate question. This is no longer simply about who you know or what you know; it's about *who knows you* and *what they know* about you.

You are probably familiar with the concept of "six degrees of separation."[2] You need to network with essentially everyone you meet because you never know who someone else knows. As previously stated, you also never know who might be able to help you further down the road.

The more people you engage through networking, the more exposure you get for your brand. Spreading your network is not just about who can help you but also who you can help. It's worth remembering that every tweet you send, every status update you make, and every picture you share (especially when you are including another person in that tweet, update, or picture and tagging it) shapes your personal brand for dozens, hundreds, or even thousands more.

Weak and Strong Ties

According to business columnist Francis Wade of The Gleaner, weak ties can be just as powerful as strong ties. So while your family and friends will always be there for you, their strong ties may not help to activate your network in the same way that weak ties (that are later transformed in to strong ties) may have a tremendous influence on your network.

In order to successfully do this, though, you will need to step out of your comfort zone. Put yourself in situations where you are making connections with people that you aren't familiar with and who belong to communities that you have never visited.[3] In today's world, doing this is a critical skill and may be the difference between getting connected to the people you want and need to connect with or remaining outside their coveted bubble. Hopefully, one day, those weak ties will become strong after all. I promise you that many of them will! In part because you boldy stepped out of your comfort zone and they will remember that!

Go Digital

LinkedIn is one of the first places that a search engine finds when searching for a person. By having a detailed and professional LinkedIn page, you assure that when potential contacts search you, the first impression you give is a memorable one.

LinkedIn is the de facto networking outlet for professionals.[4] It has become like Facebook for business—*the* place you can search similar individuals in similar industries and read their bios and accomplishments to see if they can add value to you or your career.

LinkedIn is also built into job boards. As such, you can upload your resume and link to your LinkedIn profile, which can give potential contacts and employers most of the information they would need about you in a given circumstance (without burdening them initially with too much information).

LinkedIn also works as an easily accessible resume. Everything a potential contact would want to know about you they can easily get from your profile. You can even upload your resume to your profile.

It also becomes a place to show off relevant job experience or awards and achievements. LinkedIn has become the easiest way to connect at or after conferences. Last, LinkedIn almost serves as the perfect digital personal brand brochure. Chapter 14 is devoted to effectively utilizing LinkedIn.

Hear the Message

People are always looking for compelling and interesting content. That's the great thing about podcasts. Podcasts are an increasingly popular and mainstream medium, averaging more than 39 million downloads per month. Apple's iTunes has surpassed 1-billion podcast subscriptions. Podcasts can be an important networking tool because you can actively seek out people with podcasts and ask to be interviewed.

With the surge in the number of Americans owning smartphones, podcasts are becoming a primary way Americans consume knowledge without having to tune in the radio (and deal with an avalanche of advertisements). The beauty of podcasting is that it allows consumers to handpick what they want to listen to and allows podcasters to develop a niche market.

Podcasts allow the listener to directly take in knowledge from experts. Many professionals look to podcasts as a way to establish credibility as well. However, the number one benefit to podcasts is that it gives you a platform to deliver your message. If you are on a podcast, there is a chance that 1 out of the 39 million downloads is you!

Face to Face

The internet and social media sites can be extremely helpful in assisting your career aspirations. However, being physically present at live functions and being actually seen by people of influence is critical too.

There are millions of people on the internet who can be easily forgotten following a digital correspondence. Face-to-face interactions, by stark contrast, are nearly unforgettable (or at the least will help you be remembered).

Talk to strangers at events, engage them in meaningful conversation, and follow up with them the next day. Gain a little piece of information on their life while talking to them that you can later use as a hook to jar their memory about you or the time you met and what you talked about. These weak ties could be your foot in the door to a much brighter future in a much improved network.

Be Tremendous by Building a Tremendous Network

Motivational speaker Charles "Tremendous" Jones is known for many things, including being tremendous! In his seminars, he always said, "You will be the same person you are five years from now except for the books you read and the people you meet."

While his words still hold true, the new economy requires us to go even further. Today it's not just about the books you read or the people you meet, it's also about the podcasts you listen to, the videos you watch, the mentors and coaches that you have in your life, and the workshops you attend.

If you want to build and activate your network, identify with all of the above and get to work!

Take Action

Reflect on the current state of your professional network and plan for growing it by doing the following:

1. Identify three books you would like to read that would help build your network.

2. Identify three people you could meet with that could help build your network.

3. Identify three podcasts you would like to read that would help build your network.

4. Identify three workshops, meetings, or conferences you would like to attend that would help build your network.

11.

POSITIONING: CHOOSE YOUR LANE, OWN YOUR LANE

"Positioning is not a statement about you—it's a statement that captures who you are. It's not a factual claim, but rather an emotional reason for people to want to be around you. It should capture the essence of who you are and how you have defined your personal brand."

— Jim Joseph, marketing executive and author

By now you should understand the true meaning and importance of branding when it comes to you and the future you wish to create. It's just as important to understand positioning in the context of personal branding.

As published in the first chapter of this book, Tom Peters once said, "We are CEOs of our own companies: Me Inc. To be in business today, our most important job is to be head marketer for the brand called You."

So who are *you* and what is the true meaning of positioning in the context of personal branding?

Marketing expert Jim Joseph (who is quoted at the introduction of this chapter) has stated positioning "is one of the most misunderstood principles. Even experienced marketers get it wrong and overcomplicate it."

Positioning is about **picking and owning a lane**. It's about deciding how on a daily basis you are going to leave an indelible mark on the people you come in contact with that is so powerful that those very same people will come to associate that mark with you and you alone.

About.com, when defining the idea of personal branding, ascribed that it is the process of developing a "mark" that is created around your personal name or your career. This mark is grounded in your unique perspective, education, and experience. It is the foundation for your personal positioning. This mark helps build your reputation and grow your network in a way that interests others. It compels them to seek you out for those things that make you unique.

In the broadest sense, positioning is about defining, owning, and communicating your unique value. To do this requires developing, distinguishing, and delivering your unique value in a way that is simple and easy to communicate.

So what is unique value and how is it tied to positioning?

In order to develop, distinguish, and deliver your unique value, you should have already been working on your mindset (Chapter 9) and defining your network (Chapter 10). While these are important aspects to consider, positioning is actually the foundation for all of these activities.

Again, positioning in personal branding is developing, distinguishing, and delivering your unique value. Stated simply—it's **picking a lane and owning it!**

Positioning is all about your unique perspective (how you see what you do), your unique education (how you know what you do), and your unique experience (how you deliver what you do). You must have a clear, analytical understanding of these three aspects in order to truly develop and own your lane.

Malcolm Forbes, the publisher of *Forbes* magazine, stated, "Too many people overvalue what they are not and undervalue what they are." Just like great companies have a clear and compelling position, people need a clear and compelling personal position as well. Those who do, like great companies, dominate their market.

Here's a prime example. Do you know which pizza brand claims it has "better ingredients" and "better pizza?" Of course you do. It's Papa John's. You know that fact because that's all the company talks about over and over in its consistent effort to position the brand in your mind. By doing so, you come to know that unique brand.

Papa John's is a great example of a business or brand that picked a lane and now owns it. Now, compare Papa John's highly effective marketplace positioning to that of its competitor, Domino's Pizza, a company still trying (seemingly year after year) to decide who or what exactly it is.

Lack of consistency kills companies. Similarly, a lack of consistency can do the same to a personal brand.

Unique Perspective

As discussed in Chapter 9, developing a proper mindset of awareness and control is a powerful tool that all successful people (and brands) learn to harness. Mindset influences perception and aids in the development of thoughts, theories, ideas, and imaginings that work. The way you perceive things—and the way you see what you personally do—results in how you see the world, the confidence level you have (and emit), and the quality of decision-making you exhibit.

Perspective is the lens or filter determining how you see the world and how you see yourself. Each of us has a different subjective lens through which we view the world. It's one of the biggest determining factors in what makes each of us so unique. It is the understanding of your own unique perspective that helps you articulate your unique value, which ultimately helps you to establish your position or strong point of view.

Former U.S. Senator John Sununu perhaps said it best when he said, "Perspective gives us the ability to accurately contrast the large with the small and the important with the less important. Without it, we are lost in a world where all ideas, news, and information look the same. We cannot differentiate, we cannot prioritize, and we cannot make good choices."

So where do individuals gain their unique perspective?

Individuals commonly gain perspective from past experiences, childhood upbringing, culture, faith, values, current circumstances, and character traits/genetic influences. All of this unfolds as we grow up.

Typically, three questions should be asked and answered when trying to understand and communicate our own unique perspective.

1. Where are you from? (Culture)
2. What do you believe? (Alignment with others)
3. What matters to you? (Values)

Past experiences can impact perception as those experiences were instilled in us in a manner that helps us makes sense of the world. We naturally recall those experiences when viewing a situation or establishing a relationship. Culture and values affect perception because they provide structure, guidelines, expectations, and rules that help people understand and interpret behavior. Perception guides how you are currently feeling, what you are thinking, and the activities you are doing.

Case in Point

Rick Stockstill, head football coach at Middle Tennessee State University in Murfreesboro, Tennessee, just southeast of Nashville, is known for many things. For instance, he is known for being the first quarterback to play for legendary coach Bobby Bowden when Bowden began to build his dynasty at Florida State in the 1980's. He's known for taking one of the nation's lowest APR's (the NCAA's measurement of academic progress among student-athletes) and elevating it to one of the best in the nation while coaching at MTSU, right alongside the Vanderbilts and Stanfords of the world. And he is known for how effectively he recruits and develops young people.

Where does such success and powerful branding start for Coach Stock? No surprise—it starts with his unique perspective.

The following text, pulled from Coach Stockstill's recruitment pitch, offers tremendous insight into Stockstill's filter, allowing others to understand how he sees his work as an NCAA college football coach and as a leader of young men. Enjoy!

You can know everything in the world, but if you don't know what <u>MATTERS</u>, then nothing does. As a college football coach, this is what <u>MATTERS</u> to me, our coaches, our players, and our team:

<u>Your Son Matters</u>.
Young people want to know three things.
- Who is in charge?
  - What are the standards?
  - How am I going to be held accountable?

I believe developing people starts with standards. Standards create buy-in. Buy-in defines chemistry. The development of your son though our program over these next four years will shape who he will be for the next 40 years and beyond. My first responsibility is to provide a set of standards that will help your son understand that if he wants more, he has to become more.

Making Choices Matters.

I believe that if you show me your friends, I will show you your future. The reality is we are all making choices and that with each choice comes a new set of opportunities and consequences. I want your son to learn not only **how** to make choices, but more importantly, **what** choices to make.

Problems in this country resulting from guns, drugs, and alcohol are real, and it's clear that people make poor choices when they are under the influence of any of these vices. I give our team examples of athletes that lost everything because of a poor choice, as well as examples of athletes that have won everything because they knew what decisions to make.

Getting Better Matters.

I believe we have to be better tomorrow than we are today, whether it is in the weight room, film room, classroom, practice field, study hall, or a career. The only way to get better at anything is to give greater effort and be intentional about the future you want to create.

There is no substitute for hard work. There are no shortcuts to the top. The only way I know to get better is to have a never-give-up attitude and a relentless work ethic.

Winning In ALL You Do Matters.

I believe winning off the field leads to winning on it. That means we have to win academically by going to class, study hall, and ultimately, graduating and transitioning into a professional career. We have to win by being a great example in the community with the choices we make. We have to win by being a great teammate, and by respecting and being accountable to each other. Once we do this, then winning on the field becomes easy. We win because we do things the right way both on and off the field.

Goals Matter.

You can accomplish all of your goals both on and off the field while being part of our program. I challenge our players to set high but attainable goals. Our team has a 96% graduation rate. With six bowl game appearances in nine years (and five out of the last six), we are also winning on the field. We have more than 10 players on NFL rosters. We are on television more than any other school in our conference. Why? Because we set and achieve worthy goals each and every season.

Finally, I want to coach and have people in our program that understand that all of this **MATTERS**. They are people of high character and integrity who embrace struggle and are willing to give back. They strive to be the best that they can be and they know how to use adversity to accelerate their growth. They represent themselves and their family in a positive way. And they do it because they understand it **MATTERS**.

This isn't for everyone and we understand that. It is for people that choose to be part of our team, a part of our future, and a part of the legacy we want to leave behind. It **MATTERS** to them, and it **MATTERS** to us. Period.

Coach Stockstill's unique perspective attracts both coaches and players to his program who align with his vision for success. That allows him to create a high level of accomplishment year after year. *He has picked a lane and he is owning it!*

Unique Education

The next step in understanding how to pick and own your own lane is developing, distinguishing, and communicating your unique education.

Now, mind you, we are not talking about simply having a college degree. The reality is that most everyone else competing for what you desire (a job, capital, opportunity) probably has a college degree as well. In business parlance, that's called a commodity, and being a commodity (or possessing a commodity) does not set you apart from the pack.

Education plays a vital role in the proliferation of culture and civilization. An education should develop our critical thinking skills and our manners, expose us to concepts like values, and help us define the elements of a life well lived. However, a unique education—one developed through deep personal exploration in concert with a formal education—is what produces confident leaders possessing strong points of view who form principle belief systems that allow them to excel in unique and unusual ways. Unique education helps us become sharp and on point— not just well-rounded.

Education is a tool that helps launch our journey, feeds us as we move through it, and, with cultivation and proper care, can deliver us to greatness. It is one of the most critical ingredients to enjoying a life well lived because without education it's difficult to answer questions like 'what do I owe myself, owe others, or owe the world around me?' Education is how you know what you do.

But education is more than just studying and getting good grades. Literary icon Mark Twain once said, "I have never let my schooling interfere with my education." Education is really just a means by which we discover ourselves and increase our knowledge. Education is a critical part of the development of an individual and society but it can be both formal and informal.

As such, education is the self-enlightening process. Whether it is subject education (which may cover math, science, history, or reading), spiritual education, financial education, character education, or another form of education, each form of education provides an opportunity to develop specialized, individual knowledge that can (and will) lead to higher career trajectories and, ultimately, enlightenment.

Education enables us to take in information and convert it into knowledge. Once we establish education and knowledge in our lives, we are able to create our own understanding of life and business, which empowers us to form our own opinions and understanding, then communicate and refine our strong point of view.

Education is by no means limited to lessons from textbooks. It is also found in lessons taught by life. With the proper education, we are supplied with the capability to help realize our potential, become battle tested, and learn to persevere.

Education helps eliminate confusion, fear, and doubt. An educated individual is not just content with accepting something because it is commonly accepted, but rather develops a curious mind and utilizes his or her ability to question and reason.

A unique education is an ongoing process! The more we learn, the more questions we should have. The more questions we have, the more answers we should be seeking. Understanding this concept of unique education informs us of how to discover those answers ourselves. It helps us take ideas and concepts, learn them, and turn them into our own powerful creations.

In the marketplace of ideas, this unique education is key to separating yourself from those around you. Today, employers want to know that you have market-specific knowledge, which comes from some form of education. But they also want to know that you can think outside the box and use your unique education to create impact.

As you study how to best position yourself for potential employers, have on hand in your mind three ready-made takeaways that you learned from both formal and informal education. These takeaways should illuminate what makes you unique and gives you market-specific knowledge or that makes you uniquely qualified to be selected for that given opportunity.

Unique Experience

The last piece in positioning your personal brand is cultivating this unique experience. Unique experience is how you deliver or connect to what you do.

Just like perspective and education, this element develops as a result of a long, internal process that requires time and thoughtfulness to achieve.

When reflecting on how this idea relates to positioning and personal branding, Joseph perhaps said it best when he stated, "I would argue that each of our personal brands began at birth. When mom and dad gave us a name, they unknowingly launched a new brand, the first of a lifetime of personal decisions that makes us each uniquely our own being—or brand. From that day forward, we spend our lives living up to our given name."

Joseph's notion that when we are birthed and given a name it is like the launch of a new brand for a company is right on point. From that point forward, we make millions of decisions that define who we are as individuals. Every decision we make and action we take leads us to some type of experience in life. Those decisions, over time, essentially mold our personal brand.

We choose our path of education, our life's work, our life partner, our friends, our religious beliefs, and our career decisions. All of these choices ultimately affect the experiences we encounter in life, shaping our personal brands.

Whatever the experience may be, it is important to always take things away from the experience and to learn something—whether it is about yourself or the situation. Think like a traveler collecting souvenirs to remember and cherish their experiences. Your life experiences—whether positive or negative—should and can be learning experiences. Correct the mistakes of the past and map out new game plans for the future. Have a room full of life's souvenirs to guide your next adventure!

Experiences are not only meant to live out and learn from but they should also be applied to one's personal brand. These life experiences and learning episodes are meant to be articulated and expressed to other people, as they are part and parcel to positioning your personal brand, or what imbues you with the unique perspective that others need! Become a storyteller!

The ability to articulate your experience or tell your story allows people to connect and relate to you. Your unique experience, when articulated, is incredibly valuable because it allows others to peer into your soul and, in turn, perhaps search and understand their own.

As individuals, it is important for us to be able to empathize with diverse audiences. We need to be able to understand their mind-set, their goals, their challenges, and their lifestyles if we ever expect to connect and bring value into someone else's life. In other words, our personal brand needs to connect with our target audience in a way that resonates with their own behaviors. As such, the situations we experience provide a vital path in connecting us with diverse people, as well as growing us as people.

There are five key experiences that help connect you to the outside world and build your unique experience. They are: the books you read, the people you meet, the workshops you attend, the mentors you have, and the struggles you encounter.

Reading books increases your vocabulary, helps you to comprehend better, helps you age better, and helps expand your mind. It broadens your life experience beyond what you can physically do or personally live out yourself.

The people you meet have a large influence over who you become. As the saying goes, you are the sum of the five people you spend the most time with. Therefore, meeting new people and spending time with different people is very beneficial.

Workshops teach you specific skills and improve you in some desired area.

Successful people in today's world have some type of coach or mentor. These are the people who guide you to where you want to be in life.

Last but not least, struggle makes us think better, communicate better, and make better future decisions.

These are the key ingredients to your unique experience. Note that our experiences should be looked at as identity capital. Our experiences should bring value to us and define us.

Putting it all Together

Now, can you answer these questions that may be part of your unique experience? What makes you unique and differentiates you from everyone else? What do you do naturally with ease and effectiveness?

Remember, positioning is grounded in unique value. Unique perspective, unique education, and unique experience are three pathways to understanding your unique positioning and to **picking and owning your lane**.

These elements are the extension of your personal brand. Positioning clearly defines what people or employers can and should expect to receive or experience when dealing with you. Understanding your position and leveraging it is a game changer. Your unique perspective, education, and experience complement and interact with one another.

You no doubt gain some of your unique perspective through the education you have achieved and through the life experiences you have encountered. The unique education you choose may rely on your perspective of the world and the experiences you have witnessed. Your unique experience can derive partly from your educational choices, as well as choices that were influenced by your unique perspective. Arguably, you can't have one without the other. However, without question, understanding each of these reservoirs of perspective is imperative to the process of **picking and owning your lane**.

Identifying your unique position starts with synthesizing all of these aforementioned elements and then asking yourself questions such as: Why should someone have a relationship with me? How do I deliver my value on a personal basis? How does all this make me different from my competitors? Developing your value is a process that comes from constant learning, from stepping outside of your comfort zone, and from growing as a person.

Ask yourself additional questions such as: What did I learn from this situation? How does my education, perspective, and experience shape me a person? How am I different today than I was yesterday? Delivering your value is putting it all together in an effective way that uniquely positions you. It is important to be as clear and as articulate as possible when communicating your unique value. How you choose to manage your personal brand will influence your daily leadership decisions and career management plans.

The main thing to remember in personal branding is to be yourself. Hence, the key word *unique* has a lot to do with it! Being yourself is how you will truly separate yourself from the competition and other people. This explains why positioning in personal branding is not simply perspective, education, and experience. It is "unique" perspective, "unique" education, and "unique" experience.

An article published on *Forbes.com* stated, "Leaders that have developed and are managing their personal brand are focused on simplification, creating a workplace culture where every employee is given the opportunity to advance; where teamwork is valued, and the goal is to strengthen the organization and its position in the marketplace and the industry they serve. They are able to simplify because they know themselves (their personal brand) so well."

The article goes on to explain that "Managing your personal brand is a never-ending journey of trial and error. Committing to managing your personal brand is a leap of faith. You must begin to think like an entrepreneur who is constantly in search of their leadership impact and influence. By remaining honest and true to yourself about who you are and what you represent as a leader, you will eventually discover your leadership style, the workplace culture that 'best fits' your style, and the type of people that allows your leadership to flourish."

The point is to clearly define and own a position. Create identity by better understanding the unique value you deliver, along with becoming better known and understood. Once this happens, you will find yourself saying things like "I specialize" or "I believe," and ultimately you will be able to get paid for the value you deliver.

You cannot expect others to know who you are and to understand you if you don't first have a clear and compelling position in the market that is uniquely yours. In other words, before someone buys into the dream, they have to buy into you, your brand, and the position you own in the market place.

The following are questions you should consider as you go about the process of deciding the lane you want to pick and own. These questions will help you uncover your unique perspective, education, and experience.

- Tell me about the achievement you are proudest of and why. What was the process or the steps you followed to accomplish it?
- Describe a situation where you had a task or project to complete with significant obstacles to overcome. What sacrifices did you have to make to complete it? What was the result?
- Tell me about a time when you were responsible for something that was in addition to your normal job responsibilities. Why did you assume this additional responsibility? What was the result?
- Define empathy in your own words. Tell me about a time when you have been empathetic in a business situation that resulted in a positive outcome.
- Tell me about a time when you stood alone in the face of a challenging situation. What did you do to overcome it? What did you learn?
- Tell me about a time when you lost your composure with a customer or colleague. What was the situation? What did you

do and what was the result? What did you learn from that experience?

- What are the responsibilities you handle in a given day? What do you do to ensure that they are completed in a timely manner? Describe a situation in which you had to multi-task to achieve a desired outcome.
- Tell me about a time you had to work with a difficult person. What were the issues and how did you handle it? What did you learn?
- Tell me about a time when you were in a difficult situation. How did you navigate your way through the issue? What did you learn from it?
- Tell me about a time when you had to make a difficult decision. What factors did you consider? What decision did you make? What were the results and what did you learn?
- Tell me about a time when you had to work with multiple departments or people to complete a goal or project. What was your role, and what was the outcome?
- Tell me about a situation in which you had to communicate information to an unreceptive audience. What communication media did you use to convey your message and why?
- Describe a time when your credibility was questioned. What steps did you take to address it? Tell me why it was questioned and how you dealt with the issues.
- Tell me about a time when you devised a new idea to accomplish a goal. What was the result?
- How do you organize and plan your day? Your week? Your activities and/or priorities?
- Tell me about a time when you had to work on a team to accomplish a goal. What was your role and what was the outcome?
- Tell me about a time when you had to make a decision with less than 100% of the information. How did you make the decision? What was the outcome?

Take Action

Ask yourself these important questions as part of the process of picking and owning your lane.

1. How has your unique perspective, education, and experience shaped your unique value and in turn, personal brand positioning?

2. There are several lanes from which you can choose to create and own a brand position (i.e., point of difference). Which set of questions ("stretch" situations, multi-tasking, or relationship building) are most relevant to you choosing a brand position? Why is that positioning basis relevant to you?

PART FOUR: MESSAGE— TELLING YOUR STORY

12.

THE POWER OF STORIES

"Great storytelling can make the difference between someone paying attention to you and someone just tuning you out."
—Christopher S. Penn, marketing expert

The moment a person meets another person, thoughts run through their minds about who they are, where they came from, what they know, and the value they could potentially deliver in their lives.

If you had thirty seconds in an elevator with someone who could change your life or career path, what would you say to them?

In terms of personal branding, our lives can be and should be consolidated into a simple story that we are always ready to deliver about where we are from, what we believe, and what matters to us. Our experiences help explain who we are, what we do, and why we matter to the world.

These stories can become a compelling way for others to understand us. We explain our lives to others through personal narrative. The way we frame and communicate our story impacts who we connect with, the opportunities we have a chance to be a part of, and the future we can create for ourselves.

The point of this chapter is to teach you how to tell your story, how to emotionally connect with others, and how to create interest around you so that you can grow your "personal legend," your business, and your bottom line. Let's get started.

Facts Tell, Stories Sell

Every great story starts with a typical day we live in. Then, at some point, defining moments about our lives are incorporated. The person you are speaking with, as they listen, is asking themselves, 'should I get further invested in this person's story? Or tune it out now? Furthermore, *should I continue to make an investment in this relationship?'*

Listeners may have some apprehension about going "all in" on your story because it represents possible change for them. Once they determine

ME

to connect with you, though, and decide to take the desired action of listening attentively, it is up to you to tell the stories that will make them a "vested partner" in your life.

Will they "get in the boat" with you? Remember, stories sell, while facts simply tell.

Stories Provide Points of Connection

Stories are a vehicle that take your complex journey and express it in simple terms that allow others to connect. By taking moments found in your life that are perhaps difficult to understand and relating them in story form, those people you come in contact with can gain a much better understanding of you.

As children, our parents taught us lessons through stories about experiences they had growing up. Whether we believed them or not—or even if we were just forced us to listen to stories about the good ole days! —those stories gave us clear examples of the struggles our parents faced and what they learned from their struggle.

Let's face it, life can be confusing. Making our journey simple through stories is a savvy step to connecting with others. Make it easy for others to understand you by providing the points of connection that bond you with them.

Things to consider about developing your story:

- Every story has a beginning, middle, and end.
- Every story that has a likeable character (you!) that goes through struggle, sometimes bouts of pity or fear, and, eventually, transformation.
- What is it about your journey that you want others to feel?
- What are you trying to influence them to do by telling them your story?

Stories Create Relationship

When trying to sell yourself, you can tell a person fact after fact but it probably won't resonate. A résumé tells facts, not the experiences and opportunities a person may have gone through. A story, by contrast, has twists and turns, moments of realization, and theme.

154

Straight to the point facts may be useful when trying to explain yourself and answer the basic who, what, when, where, and why questions regarding your life or situations you have been in. However, facts aren't memorable like stories are.

Telling a story creates curiosity. It keeps the listener interested in what is going to happen next. Stories rely on anticipation, not, as a policeman or lawyer might say, "just the facts." Stories tease people along, raise (and eventually, in good time, answer) questions in people's minds, and keep prospects hooked to see where the story will lead next.

And, in fact, a key to storytelling is that people always want to know what happens next. They are wired for interest in outcomes and each step along the way that that led to getting there. How life unfolds is endlessly fascinating to people because they have had similar experiences in their own lives.

Relating to your audience is also key to great storytelling. Johnny Cash, the famous country singer and songwriter, was able to use one phrase, "I shot a man in Reno, just to watch him die" to captivate an audience of unruly prison inmates during a jailhouse concert. When your story relates to your audience, they are eager to hear what you have to say. They hang on your every word. The audience begins to feel a connection with you and that connection is what allows you to begin to build a real relationship.

Stories Help Fight the Resistance

Is your guard up when first meet somebody? Naturally. Whether it is for an interview, talking to a crowd of unknown faces, or meeting for a first date, people are intrinsically afraid of being taken advantage of or looking foolish in front of others. That's why most people tread lightly in a new relationship. You need trust and to sense authenticity in a person before you can loosen up and essentially invite them in to your world.

How do you build trust and reveal authenticity? When there is a story involved, there is little to resist. That's because in storytelling, you are not simply telling people what you think, you are showing them what happened in a similar situation as they might have faced, then leaving it up to them to draw their own conclusions about your choices and character.

Jonah Sachs, a great American storyteller, once stated, "Human beings share stories to remind each other of who they are and how they should behave. When we hear stories based on these patterns, we feel more like we're remembering something forgotten than learning something new."

Great stories resonate. Great storytellers know their audience so they increase their chances of their stories resonating. And resonating results in relationships.

Stories Make It Personal

Paulo Coelho, author of *The Alchemist* wrote, "Discovering, honoring, and fulfilling our personal legend is the only job we have." Think back to elementary school where the "Legend of You" began. Remember when you met your future best friends for the first time? How did you decide who you were going to be friends with? I'm guessing you talked to and got to know all of your other classmates for a little while. You would hear each of their "stories" and you would sift through them in your mind making a connection with one person over another based on where they came from and what their story revealed (and how it resonated with you).

Given you were in elementary school, the stories probably weren't deep or very well thought out with an intention to sell you on something; but I'll bet they were genuine and gave you a real sense of who each person was (and who you wanted to spend more time with).

When using stories to connect with others, find a way to make it personal. How? Use obstacles you might have faced in your life or victories you might have had from time to time to relate to personal experiences your listeners might have been through too. Once they hear your personal stories, they will think to themselves, 'you know what, this person understands what I have been through.' They begin to trust in what you are saying. And with that affirmation of your character, you gain their respect and attention.

People want to listen to someone they relate with on deeper levels than just work or small talk. They want someone that "gets it" —and where the "it" is them!

Know Your Audience

The better you know your audience the, more effectively you can create appealing content ideas, make decisions on story formats, handle positioning and placement in your stories, and promote your content. If you can put yourself in the shoes of your customer, you know precisely what they want and what it will take for them to be engaged in your content. Ultimately it is the audience that matters. It's up to you to find out what they want or need.

Now, it's time to give thought to how stories should be presented to an audience. Lay them out from beginning, to middle, to buildup, and finally, to ending:

- Start at the beginning. A great story gives the other person a chance to see what you perceive as base-line reality and decide if they agree with your initial perception.
- The middle of your story should paint the picture of the actual state versus the ideal state that we wish was happening, then point directly to where the gap is. Your audience may see themselves in that gap!
- The buildup of your story should be focused on the transformation. The old saying is that people and organizations change for two reasons: pain or potential. They either see themselves with so much pain that they have to change or they see themselves with so much potential that they know they can achieve it. Which relates to your story?
- Your ending should be about the new opportunity that is created together. It's something your audience has to see and feel. It's called "being in the boat" with the client or the audience.

A winning theme is that you went through struggle and yet found a way to cross over to the other side and survived and learned from your experience, were transformed along the way, and now tell your story because you realize that your struggle helped you think better, communicate better, and make better decisions. Your audience will resonate with a story like that!

Use Questions to Craft Your Story

Dig into the "real you" to find elements of your personal journey that would make for interesting stories that sell Brand You. Ask yourself the following questions as you create stories based on your unique perspective, education, and experience:

- What or who inspired you?
- Why do you care about what you care about?
- Discuss your unique perspective, or how you see what you do. Why is that important?
- What is "cool" about you?
- What are some moments pulled from your educational experiences (both formal and informal) that make you unique?
- What struggles have you faced and overcome in your life journey?
- What sacrifices have you made?
- Have you ever been motivated by pain or potential? Both? When?
- What is your vision for life?
- What are some unexpected events in your life or business career that led to greater opportunity?
- What makes your experience or how you connect to the world unique?

Story Types

Telling stories that reflect the Meaning and Makeup of your personal brand need not follow a single method or pattern. You have some leeway in crafting personal Here are some options:

- *"Claim, Explain, Example" stories.* When you state an idea or use a concept, finish the thought with, "So, for example…" or "Here is the point…" to guide your listener along the way. Then give specific examples related to the client or audience. This helps provide clarity, focus, and direction to your storytelling.

- *Ten Road Blocks.* List the 10 greatest road blocks that you experienced in your life and give them one word titles. Turn those 10 words into 10 vignettes. Include enough detail so you can read the description months later and remember the story well enough to tell it in a compelling way over and over again in ad lib fashion.

- *Unique Perspective Stories.* These help you get others to see a situation from a different perspective, without coming across as elitist.

- *Unique Education and Experience Stories.* These stories help you communicate exactly how (through your education and experiences) you added value with *other* clients or audiences. The goal is to get the client or audience to imagine themselves connecting to you in the same way!

- *Pain/Potential Stories.* Describe "before and after" stories of the pain, concluding with the "after picture" of the resulting positive outcomes.

The moment a person meets another person, thoughts run through their minds about who they are, where they came from, what they know, and the value they could potentially deliver in their lives. What will you say to them?

Take Action

1. Look at your résumé and think about each information point you have listed (education, experience, volunteerism, etc.). What are the three most compelling stories you can associate to these three items on your résumé?

2. Apply the Ten Road Blocks story structure and write it out. This technique is a building block toward communicating your Meaning and Makeup. Which three personal road blacks have the greatest appeal to the widest range of audiences?

13.

GET SOCIAL

"Social media is the ultimate equalizer. It gives a voice and a platform to anyone willing to engage."
—Amy Jo Martin

Social Media: The Corner Pub Meets the Office Water Cooler

The above statement by social media expert Amy Jo Martin sums up the power of social media. It is an equalizer that offers a platform from which to be recognized and heard.

Social media amplifies your voice by allowing you to craft a presence for your brand through words, photos, and video. If you think about it, in the age of social media, the ability to tell your brand story is no longer constrained geographically. Your access stretches around the entire globe.

Social media also amplifies your voice through its ability to connect you directly with hiring managers, potential mentors, or other professionals positioned to benefit you (and for you to benefit them).

It's almost hard to remember a time (and some younger readers may never have experienced it), but before electronic communications came along, networking was by necessity done either face-to-face, by telephone, or, yes, by postal mail. The higher level of difficulty involved in connecting with influential people made it much easier for gatekeepers (read: secretaries, assistants, or public relations reps) to prevent access and therefore connections from occurring.

Those days are obviously over. Today, social media makes it quite easy to bypass gatekeepers, as many of the professionals with whom you seek to engage have a highly visible, open, and inviting presence on social networking sites.

The rise of social media as a communication channel brings with it not just opportunities but also challenges to building your personal brand as well. Perhaps the main challenge is finding the right mix of social networking sites on which you should have a brand presence. Hundreds of online social networking sites exist, so the question becomes which ones are best suited for building your professional network (part of brand Makeup) with the people in the professions you seek to enter? Or which sites have active communities of users with whom you can give of yourself and build relationships through the act of networking?

When you boil it down, two types of social networking sites exist: mass audience networks and niche networks. The best combination or mix of social channels for a particular individual depends largely on their profession or interest area.

The following offers an overview of how social networking sites can be used to manage the Message aspect of your personal brand.

Mass Audience Social Networks

Mass audience social network sites attract a large audience because they have a wide range of content appealing to people with varied interests. Although subjects on mass audience networks can still attract narrow audiences through (for instance) groups on Facebook or hashtags on Twitter, these networks generally attract users across essentially large and nebulous demographic and psychographic market segments.

Five mass audience social networks that can be valuable for your brand Message, though, are discussed here: Facebook, Twitter, Instagram, Pinterest, and Google+. A sixth network is so important in managing brand Message that it is the sole focus of Chapter 14: LinkedIn.

The extent to which each of these mass audience networks can benefit you specifically varies by profession and in relation to your communication objectives. Use the overview of the five key social networks as a starting point to begin exploring whether or not they are right for you.

Facebook

Before you dismiss Facebook as exclusively a place for keeping up with your friends (and for your parents to keep up with you and your friends), consider several compelling reasons why Facebook could be a useful tool for personal branding:

Marketing via your profile. The first step you should take to get Facebook working for you as a personal branding tool is to build out your profile to reflect the authentic you—Meaning, Makeup, and Message. Your interests—places visited, favorite movies, sports allegiances, top-rated music and books—all reflect your values, purpose, and passions (Meaning). Work and education histories provide a quick glimpse of your skills and experience (Makeup). Links to where you can be found on other social networks provide people with a portal to learn more about you and also to connect with you in other places (Message). Think of your Facebook profile as being like a résumé and you will be imminently more thoughtful and deliberate in the content that you include (and omit) from your profile.

Targeting opportunities. Did you know that 65% of recruiters use Facebook to find and evaluate job candidates?[1] Recruiters, hiring managers, and employees at businesses and organizations of interest to you are most certainly using Facebook to sift through candidates. Segment your friends on Facebook (e.g., school acquaintances, family, industry organizations and companies, and professional contacts). Segmenting contacts in this way will enable you to target content to audiences that you want to impress with useful material that reflects your interest in and knowledge of a particular field. Another benefit of segmenting your Facebook friends is to exclude recipients from content that you prefer not to share with all of your friends or the public.

Networking. Think of Facebook's news feed as a channel for you to share content related to your professional interests. Links to articles, blogs, websites, and videos are examples of content you might post to a segmented friends list. Posting relevant content for an audience of people with similar professional or subject interests enables you to demonstrate you have your "head in the game" and strengthens your association in the minds of people in professional fields (artists, bankers, etc.) to which you aspire to belong. This subtly feeds your expert status. Be deliberate in sharing content in terms of quality and quantity, though. The number one reason Facebook users unfriend others is due to the posting of what they consider to be offensive content. Of course, you are not embarking on the journey of personal branding to upset people in the very community in which you aspire to be a member! So don't let sensitive content that you post (especially content unrelated to the community's main interests) be a reason people do not want to connect with you on Facebook.

To successfully use Facebook as part of your brand Message strategy, you must really use it! It is not enough to just set up an account, complete your profile, and occasionally post (or worse yet, just "stalk"). Two additional reasons Facebook users most often choose to unfriend others is that they do not know someone on their friends list very well, or a person does not interact with them (or on Facebook in general) very often.[2] Being a community member on a social network like Facebook can be fulfilling in that you receive benefits of knowledge and connections, but you must give as well as receive! The giving/receiving line, though, is a fine one. If you don't post often, you can become "invisible" to others and could be unfriended. On the other hand, posting too much or content sharing to excess (particularly if that content comes across as heavy self-promotion) can be a strong turnoff that prompts users to unfriend you.

If the thought of having to post content to attract or keep friends on Facebook sounds a bit intimidating, remember that there are two other ways to give: leaving comments on other people's posts and sharing others' posts. Think of commenting and sharing as the "social" aspect of social media coming into play. Show your appreciation to friends when they post useful content by liking it, sharing it with your friends (being sure to acknowledge the original poster), and/or leaving comments to express your opinion or appreciation for the content that was shared.

Advertise. No, you did not misread this—you can use Facebook to advertise your personal brand. Placing ads is rare compared to the other four reasons for using Facebook for managing brand Message, but it is an option. Just as companies and products use paid message placement to gain attention in your news feed, you can craft an ad that is targeted to a specific geographic market, industry, or company. You set a daily budget for the maximum you want to spend. Facebook ads can be used to gain attention, stand out from the large majority of your competition that is not utilizing Facebook ads, and direct recipients to your website, blog, or other destination where they can learn more about you. Facebook ads may not lead directly to landing your desired job, but it can widen your exposure, build networking contacts, and gain feedback from others on how to achieve your job search goals.[3]

Twitter

Facebook may be the social network of choice in terms of sheer number of users, but do not discount Twitter as valuable channel for personal brand building.

First of all, a lot of people are on Twitter—19% of adult online users have Twitter accounts. The age groups with the highest percentages of Twitter users are 18-29 year-olds (35%) and 30-49 year-olds (20%)[4]. Second, Twitter is a social network used a great deal by individuals and organizations. Today, Twitter has more than 300 million monthly active users spread across the globe.[5]

Like most other social networks, much of the content posted to Twitter does not pertain to work—it is more often than not leisurely chatter and conversation about TV shows, sporting events, or political candidates—the kinds of topics people generally like to talk about around the proverbial water cooler. Because of that, even if you are a regular Twitter user, you may not be familiar with just how successfully it can be used as a resource in your professional life.

Twitter can be valuable for your brand Makeup through learning from content shared by others and through expanding the number and quality of individuals and organizations in your professional network. The Message dimension of your personal brand can be boosted by using Twitter to engage with other people in conversations and information sharing (networking practices). It can also help shape the perceptions others hold about your brand (such as your expertise and personality) as a residual of the type, tone, and value of the content you post (brand Message priorities).

New Twitter users will quickly recognize its most unique characteristic: a 140-character maximum on posts. While it might seem limiting at first to confine yourself to such short posts, you will come to adapt to and even embrace the format. Besides, many tweets are often used to link users to longer-form content such as a blog post or video, a scenario in which a short-hand introduction or appetizer serves its purpose well. Twitter offers advice to new users on getting started. Like any other new tool you choose to use, the key to becoming better at it is practice.

Let's drill down past the white noise that you can also find readily available on Twitter to get to the most beneficial uses of the tool for personal branding. Three valuable Twitter features you can utilize are lists, hashtags, and chats.

Lists. The default connection between two parties on Twitter is that you can follow another account without consent, or, follow back from the other party (that is, unless a user has his or her tweets protected, meaning approval must be granted by that party in order for you to follow). As such, you can set out to target users in specific industries, companies, or cities, just to name three possible segmentation options. More importantly, take advantage of Twitter's list function to segment accounts that you follow. Twitter allows you to have up to 1,000 different lists with a maximum of 5,000 users followed in a given list, which is more than enough capability to create finely segmented lists.

What is the advantage of creating lists? It sorts content being posted by the accounts you follow into separate "buckets." That way, rather than scrolling through your timeline, you can make your time spent on Twitter more efficient by reading, replying, retweeting, and liking, etc., only to content pertaining to a specific focus. For example, if you aspire to work in public relations, you can create a list of Twitter users that blog about PR, are PR professionals, or are affiliated with public relations industry organizations or PR agencies. Twitter gives easy-to-follow guidance on how to create lists and add/delete users from lists. It should be noted that you do not have to follow a user to include them in a list (although you can if you wish).

Hashtags. Another powerful feature of Twitter is the hashtag. The purpose of hashtags is to make tweets more searchable by relating a tweet's content or theme to a topic, current event, or other unifying concept. Use hashtags to target content you post, as well as to pinpoint tweets that are potentially of interest to you. If you have an interest in financial markets, you might follow hashtags such as #NYSE, #NASDAQ, and #SP500 that will direct tweets to you marked with these hashtags. Likewise, you can share information with others by using hashtags to identify the subject or focus of your own tweets. Finally, in addition to helping to filter tweets to match your interests, using hashtags enables you to discover people and organizations that post valuable content to Twitter and to add them to lists (or follow them) so that you continue to receive the value from their future tweets. If you are new to Twitter or have not tried using hashtags, check out a hashtag directory like Twubs to find established hashtags. Alternately, you can use a trial and error approach by simply typing terms into Twitter's search feature (e.g., #personalbranding) to see what content is being shared using that hashtag.

Chats. One of the most appealing aspects of Twitter is its real-time communication functionality. Conversations occur on the spot, not only between two individuals, but also among a large group of users when a hashtag is used to "brand" the conversation. As a result, Twitter chats have emerged as a virtual meet-up for people with shared interests. These chats are useful for learning, networking, and demonstrating expertise. Do you work in sports business or want to break into that field? You will likely benefit from checking out the weekly chats #sbchat (sports business) and #smsportschat (social media in sports). A typical Twitter chat is held weekly on the same day and time (usually lasting one hour). A hashtag is created for the chat that is used each time a chat session occurs.

Best of all, Twitter chats can be found for any topic or subject that is interesting enough for Twitter users to invest time in. If you have not tried taking part in a Twitter chat before, once again refer to the chat directory website Twubs for a schedule of chats. If you do not see one that fits your interest area, guess who can start one? Yes, you! Another way you can find out about chats is from tweets posted by users that you are following. If you cannot "attend" the chat due to schedule conflict, no worries—search the hashtag for the chat to read tweets posted during the session. Also, many Twitter chat organizers post a transcript of each session that you can refer to anytime.

Instagram

While Instagram is thought of primarily as a photo sharing site, consider for a moment the scope of possibilities it holds as a visual medium benefitting your brand Message.

The percentage of adult Internet users with Instagram accounts is only slightly less than the percentage with Twitter accounts (17% have Instagram, while 19% have Twitter), but Instagram users are very active— 500 million monthly active users worldwide that post 95 million photos/videos daily.[6] The typical Instagram user is also an engaged user; an astounding 8,500 likes and 1,000 comments *per second* occur on

Instagram. More evidence of audience engagement is that 43% of users post more than once daily.[7] These eye-popping statistics defining Instagram's audience size and engagement levels suggests it is too attractive of a channel to not consider as a key part of the Message platform for your personal brand.

Whether you are already one of the engaged users reflected in the statistics above or are just now considering testing the Instagram waters, consider these three ways Instagram can be employed to jumpstart your brand building:

Share your authentic brand. Your professional life is but one component of the "total you," meaning it does not tell your complete story. Use Instagram to give users a glimpse into other aspects of your life that complement your professional existence, whether they be hobbies, vacations, or amusing observations—essentially the activities and interests that represent who you really are. Of course, use Instagram to share photos in a professional context as well, such as when you attend a conference or networking event. The point here is to resist the idea of making all of your content exclusively revolve around your professional life.

Use hashtags to build awareness. Like Twitter, hashtags on Instagram aid users in sorting through the avalanche of content available to find photos that relate specifically to their interests. Be strategic in using hashtags. Experts suggest focusing on five to ten hashtags to associate with your brand (your company, a slogan, industry, or subject are examples). Consistently include relevant hashtags with your posts to reach an audience beyond your current crop of followers. This tactic can lead to expanding your network by attracting people with whom you might not otherwise connect through hashtags.

Engage, engage, engage. Posting photos and making use of hashtags will in all likelihood yield more followers for you, but they will not remain connected to you if you do not engage them going forward. Just as using hashtags related to important aspects of your brand Meaning and Makeup will attract new followers, you will also discover people and brands to follow because their use of hashtags speaks in a relevant manner to you. Whether users are finding you or you are finding users to follow, take time to engage by liking others' photos, making comments, asking questions, and following users that you find interesting or who offer useful content.

Pinterest

Another visually dominant social network that holds great potential for communicating brand Message is Pinterest.

Like Instagram, Pinterest launched in 2010 and quickly became a go-to social network, especially for women. It is estimated that at least 80% of Pinterest's 40 million monthly active users in the United States are female.

If you are male, do not let this statistic discourage you from having a personal brand presence on Pinterest. What is most important in deciding whether to use Pinterest (or any communication channel) is who you are trying to attract or reach to engage with your brand. If that audience uses Pinterest, you should be a participant in that community, regardless of your personal gender.

Pinterest activity is centered on "pinning" content to boards you create that enable you to organize and present content by subject or theme. So how does Pinterest help manage your brand Message? Consider these benefits:

Share your authentic brand. Just as posting photos to Instagram can give users insight into both your professional and personal interests, your Pinterest boards can have the same effect. You probably do not lead a one-track life; you may be a student that studies architecture, dabbles in making craft beer, plays golf on weekends, or are a classic movie buff, for example. As such, you could create Pinterest boards around each of these themes in your life, having the sum effect of expressing both your professional and personal interests. You will build a following not only by offering value through content pinned to your professional interests, but others will follow you because they have similar outside pursuits, or simply find you and your content to be interesting.

Be a resource for others. Build-out your presence on Pinterest by pinning content you find online. Photos, articles, videos, blog posts—each of these are the types of content you come across while using the Internet for research and learning that can be added (or pinned) to boards you create.

169

Of course, original content that you create can be pinned to your boards, too. Another way your Pinterest presence can become a resource for others is when you re-pin content you find valuable to your boards. Just don't forget to show some love to the original pinner by commenting on and liking the pin! This practice will not only help you build a larger following, but add value for others by curating interesting content on your personal boards.

Show your work. Many people believe there is a fine line between showing your capabilities and self-promotion. If you are too reserved in posting your original writings, photos, videos, recipes, illustrations, etc., you are denying a larger audience the utility or enjoyment that can be found in your work. For example, if you are an interior designer, showcase client projects you have performed by having a Projects board and pinning to it. If you are an interior design student, pin samples of creative work from class projects. Other users might be inspired by your ideas, which can lead to expanding your network of contacts, or, perhaps even to job opportunities. Be sure not to limit the showcasing of good works, though, exclusively to your own creations. Balance featuring your content with others' work that you admire. If you focus predominantly on sharing your work with little acknowledgement of useful content being shared by others, you run the risk of being deemed a self-promoter who is only out to benefit him or herself. Strike a balance. Showcase your great work. But be a community participant as well and engage other users and their great works to show appreciation for a wide variety of content. Use Pinterest as an online portfolio to communicate your value.

Google+

A fifth mass audience social networking site to include in the mix as you build up your Message platform is Google+.

Opinions on the usefulness of Google+ are wide ranging (as are predictions about its future). Depending on whose opinion you wish to believe, Google+ is either a ghost town nearing collapse or an indispensable tool necessary for the health and wealth of your digital presence.

Although Google+ does not have the cultural significance of Facebook or the trendiness of Twitter, Instagram, or Pinterest, it does have something very valuable: namely, a large audience. Google+ has more than 340 million active monthly users.[8] As with any social network, the extent to which Google+ is used by professionals in a given field or industry varies, so you will want to research how it is being utilized by people and companies in your interest area to gauge its potential for you.

As you evaluate the utility of Google+, consider four potential benefits for personal branding:

Reaching. Google+ has one advantage that no other social networking site can offer: It's Google! Approximately two-thirds of all queries typed into search engines online occur on Google. Content posted and shared through your Google+ presence is indexed by the Google search engine, just as it is done for any website. This characteristic means that people could come across your brand simply as a result of your efforts to create and share content that is relevant to others. Think of Google+ as possessing tremendous search engine optimization (SEO) benefits for your personal brand, potentially moving you higher in search engine results.

Targeting. Like other social networking sites, Google+ allows you to segment your network of connections. The Circles feature of Google+ lets you construct targeted lists of people or organizations you wish to follow. You can segment your network by friends, classmates, professional colleagues, local connections, or any other category you wish to utilize. In turn, you can target content posted or shared to a specific circle or circles. *Networking*. Google+ enables users to connect with others sharing similar interests: through the Communities features Google+ Communities are just that, groups of people drawn together by a similar profession or passion. Communities can be public or private and can be created by anyone... including you! Any community member can post content or start discussions.

Learning. Google+ Collections organize the vast content of Google+ into focused topics. Collections relate to nearly any imaginable interest- work, play, and more! You can follow collections curated by other users, or you can curate your own collection that can be followed by others sharing your interest.

Niche Social Networks

While mass audience networks are immediately associated with social media, these mass audience networks are relatively few in number. Meanwhile, more than 300 social networking websites exist. The large majority of them fall into the category of niche networks.

Niche social network sites are websites whose content appeals to a narrow group of people based on their demographic characteristics or interests. Although mass audience social network sites have the power to attract people with shared interests, the appeal of niche networks is that their dedicated platforms have the potential to meet the needs and desires of users more effectively than a mass audience network. For example, deviantART is a niche social network where users can view and download art, submit works in contests, and discuss art with fellow art lovers. devinatART is typical of what niche social networks' can provide.[9] Figure 13.1 gives examples of niche social networks and their content focus.

Social Network	Description
Quora	A forum for asking questions and answering questions of other users on a wide range of topics
Meetup	An event directory in a local area for professional interests, skills, or hobbies useful for learning and networking
Care2	Its tagline "the world's largest community for good" sums up members' aims- promoting philanthropic causes and environmentally sustainable practices
Book-in-a-Week	A community for writers that shares resources, offers motivational prompts, issues writing challenges, and builds comradery among writers
Behance	A showcase of creative works (graphic design, photography, art, illustrations); Users promote their works to get hired or be recommended for hire

Figure 13.1 Examples of Niche Social Networking Sites

The difference between mass audience and niche networks is analogous to the way broadcast and cable television networks work. Like broadcast television networks such as ABC, NBC, and Fox, mass audience social media networks have content that appeals to a wide audience; virtually all topics and interests are fair game on sites like YouTube, for example. In contrast, niche social media networks are more like History, Lifetime, or the Golf Channel. Content is targeted to specific audiences and their interests. Like their cable television counterparts, niche social network sites have smaller audiences, although the people who are drawn to these niche networks tend to be highly involved with the content themes of the network. Thus, they are likely to interact with the network more frequently (more site visits) and spend more time on the site.

Mind Your Social Media Manners

As previously stated, social networking sites have, without question, amplified voices like never before. That amplification, however, can be either good or bad for the voices being amplified.

It is probably safe to say that no one sets out to sabotage their personal brand through social media blunders. However, that's exactly what can happen and does happen on a daily basis.

When a person is careless, or even momentarily drops his or her guard and posts content that is offensive or distasteful, the result can be permanently damaging to brand reputation. One survey of hiring managers found that 43% of them were influenced to not hire an applicant because of troublesome content posted on his or her social media pages, including racy photos, intolerance, photos showing alcohol consumption, and misrepresenting credentials.[10]

On a positive note, findings from the same survey indicated that 20% of hiring managers selected candidates *because of* content they found posted on social media profiles, offering further evidence that what you say and do on social media can work to your advantage.

What are the keys to unlocking social media's potential to bolster your brand? Regardless of which social networking sites you choose to establish a presence on, make the following actions priorities:

Listen. If you are new to a particular social networking site or do not feel very confident in your ability to use social media to communicate your brand Message, start by making it a point to listen (read) what others are saying. Build confidence by providing feedback to others in the form of likes, comments, or questions.

Share. As your comfort level grows, add value to others in your networks by sharing content you find useful, be it quotes, articles, infographics, or videos. One of the main benefits of networking with others is the discovery of new and fresh ideas and inspiration made possible when we share with each other.

Tell. Building your brand using social media should not center on selling yourself or your products. That said, a failure to sell yourself by telling stories that represent your brand is a huge missed opportunity as well. If you spend time on social media, you likely have encountered people who stray across that fine line between selling themselves through adding value and simple self-promotion. Always remember that when you give to people (meaning attention through listening or knowledge through sharing), you add value and earn the right to "get" (meaning to tell the benefits of your brand and how you add value to others).

Take Action

Take the following actions or ask yourself these important questions before we proceed with the process of building your personal brand:

1. Rank the five mass audience social networking sites discussed in this chapter (Facebook, Twitter, Instagram, Pinterest, and Google+) in terms of their potential to strengthen the Makeup and Message dimensions of your personal brand, with 1 being the most important site, 2 the next most important, and so on. Then, focus on the networking site you ranked number 1. On a scale from 1 to 10, with 1 being "very ineffective" and 10 being "very effective," rate your current use of this social networking site for enhancing your brand Makeup and Message.

    If your rating is 1-9, identify how you could improve your use of this social networking site for personal branding. If your rating is a 10, identify what you do that makes this site such a strength for you. If you are not presently active on the social networking site you ranked 1st, identify obstacles preventing you from being an active user of the site.

2. Consider whether niche social networking sites have potential benefit in building your personal brand. If you are familiar with a niche social network (whether you are an active user on it or not), how could participation in that community benefit your personal brand? If you are unfamiliar with niche social networks that might be relevant to you, research whether or not one exists.

    If you are unable to find a niche network related to your field, consider how a niche network that pertains to diverse interests like Meetup could benefit your personal brand development instead. Should a niche social networking site be part of your brand Message platform? Why or why not?

14.

LINKEDIN: A LEAGUE OF ITS OWN

"Active participation on LinkedIn is the best way to say 'Look at me!' without saying 'Look at me!'"
—Bobby Darnell, management consultant

Each of the social networking sites discussed in Chapter 13 offers solid contributions to the Message dimension of your personal brand. There is one social network, however, that is the social network king of the personal brand building space: LinkedIn.

LinkedIn is often referred to as "Facebook for business," and while that analogy is useful for people unfamiliar with LinkedIn, a closer look at its functions reveal even more unique benefits for your professional identity.

LinkedIn actually launched before Facebook, making its debut in 2003. It has more than 450 million members worldwide, with over 125 million U.S. users alone. Although LinkedIn's user base is massive already, the company has even more ambitious plans: a goal of 3 billion users worldwide.[1]

As LinkedIn has evolved, it has enabled businesses and organizations to establish a presence, too. More than 4 million companies now also have pages on LinkedIn. Companies clearly see the value in using LinkedIn to market their brands to prospective customers and employees.

Are there millions of individuals attempting to promote themselves using LinkedIn? Yes, there are. However, there are not just "sellers" on LinkedIn; there are many "buyers," too.

One estimate of recruiting activity states one out of every 20 profiles on LinkedIn belongs to a recruiter.[2] That's good news for job seekers. Of course, that also means that 19 out of 20 LinkedIn profiles belong to a person who might not be looking to recruit employees and is instead on LinkedIn for the same reasons you should be—to learn, to build a network of professionals with shared interests, and yes, to promote yourself.

Given the essential nature of LinkedIn, it is appropriate for us to take a deep dive into how to get the most out of LinkedIn in the areas of promotion, networking, and learning.

Promotion

The most obvious use of LinkedIn for anyone is promoting their brand, be it as a student preparing to launch a career, someone in search of a new job, or someone already established in a career but desiring to create an improved presence among peers in their company or industry.

As with any social networking site, it is important not to cross the line between effective self-marketing and shameless self-promotion. Remember that you are a member of a community, so be generous in giving back to that community through re-posts, likes, shares, and comments. With that understood, be diligent in positively promoting your brand through two important LinkedIn features: profile and publishing.

Your Profile

The most critical piece of your LinkedIn presence is creating and managing your profile. After all, it is the first contact people have with you on LinkedIn, whether they are searching for you or just discover you under the "People You May Know" tab on the Home page.

Your profile serves the same functions as a business card and résumé—identifying you quickly and succinctly and summarizing who you are. The content in your profile, therefore, can heavily influence whether you are noticed or ignored by the people who encounter your page. Make your profile work for you by caring for it constantly–lest we forget it is for the world's most important brand! You!

The elements of your profile include headline, photo, summary, experience, honors and awards, skills and endorsements, and recommendations.

Headline. The first bits of information that one receives about you on LinkedIn comes from your headline. Like a headline for a newspaper article, the length of your LinkedIn headline must be short, as in no more than 120 characters. Use this limited space to your advantage in order to get attention. Think about how your headline could stand out amid a sea of sameness.

Executive recruiter Pete Leibman gives four solid suggestions for writing an effective headline:

- *Avoid "cheesy" words and phrases*—You may work in the words social media marketing among your abilities, but please do not call yourself a "guru" or a "rock star." A search for "social media guru" on LinkedIn returned more than 1,700 results, which is a lot of gurus for such a relatively new field...and you will likely never see a job posting in which a company wants to hire a guru! Instead, communicate your value more specifically by using a moniker like "Facebook marketing specialist."

- *Avoid confusing words and phrases*—If your official title or role is not easily understood, consider using different wording to convey your value. For example, if your current title is "Engagement Manager," it would probably be better to restate using more easily understood terms what exactly you do in terms of your job function or the benefit you deliver to your customers or organization.

- *Avoid boring words and phrases*—What happens when a headline in a newspaper or magazine fails to grab your attention? You skip the content that follows and move on. Similarly, a boring headline in your profile could lead to the same result. The simplest approach to crafting a catchy headline is to give a straightforward description of what you do (e.g., tax accountant) or your current status (e.g., student), then segue to a statement or phrase that captures or suggests the value you offer. In the case of a student, then, perhaps write a headline that lets others know of your desired professional destination, such as "aspiring pharmaceutical sales professional." That gives a much clearer and immediate picture of who you are now and how you wish to position yourself in the business world after graduation.

- *Avoid sounding desperate (even if you are!)*—If you are looking for a job or find yourself unexpectedly seeking a new career opportunity, it is advisable not to use the descriptors "unemployed" or "seeking new opportunity" in your headline. Instead, use words that communicate past results or your credentials. Otherwise, people may focus more attention on questioning why you are unemployed rather than on your capabilities for openings.[3]

Photo. Along with the headline, your photo is important for getting attention, and, more importantly, engaging potential connections. The default photo image is a silhouette. That's not adequate. Be prepared to upload a photo as soon as you build your profile. Even without ever having laid eyes on you, it is a certainty that you are more attractive, personable, and engaging than the faceless outline that is the LinkedIn default photo! That said, take care not to upload just any old photo that is conveniently accessible on your computer or smartphone. Specifically, the photo you use for your profile should meet the following criteria:

- *Use the right size image*—Minimum image size is 200 x 200 pixels; maximum is 500 x 500 pixels.

- *Dress in the attire that is the norm in your industry*—Although it is unlikely that anyone would be accused of being overdressed if wearing traditional business attire in a profile photo, it is acceptable to wear what others in your field wear. Avoid using photos in which you are not wearing appropriate business attire— meaning those photos you might have saved from your recent family reunion where you were dressed in your t-shirt and baseball cap! Such photos are generally not suitable for LinkedIn no matter how good you think you might be looking in them.

- *Use a photo of you and only you*—Your profile photo should not be a cropped image of a photo of you with one or more other people (even if you are dressed appropriately in it). A photo of you with someone else's hand draped around your neck or flowing hair appearing around your shoulder also serves to distract the viewer and is generally viewed as unprofessional in nature.

- *Use a professional looking headshot*—Many experts encourage a professional headshot. While that is ideal, it need not be taken by a professional photographer. Just be sure that the photographer you enlist for help is not you (meaning no selfies!). What is important is that it meets the above criteria.

The motivation to carefully select a profile photo that meets these four criteria is simple. Not unlike on dating websites, profiles with a photo are 14 times more likely to be viewed and explored than ones without one.[4]

You can also upload a background image to enhance the visual appeal of your profile. This might be a photo of you in action (making a presentation, working at your desk, etc.) that further expresses who you are professionally speaking. Minimum image size for a background photo is 1000 x 425 pixels. Maximum size is 4000 x 4000 pixels.

Summary. Relatively few people write autobiographies, but the summary section of your LinkedIn profile enables you to do just that—write the "story of you" in 2,000 characters or less.

If the emphasis of your headline and photo is to grab attention, then the summary is your first real chance to engage prospective LinkedIn connections at a deeper level. The content of your summary should be like effective copy in a print advertisement, meaning it communicates the benefits of "Brand You" through your Meaning and Makeup attributes, offers evidence of performance capabilities, and compels the reader to want to take action—namely, to connect with you.

Given the importance of writing an appealing summary, what are the keys to success? Personal branding expert William Arruda says the process for a well-written summary entails the following:

- *Ask yourself what you want to communicate through your summary*—This step entails asking three questions: Who do you want to reach (i.e., your target audience)? What do you want them to learn or do after reading the summary? And how do you want them to feel? The answers to these questions will make it easier to complete the next two steps in crafting a summary section.

- *Gather content*—The heart of your summary is the "story of you," meaning descriptions of your passions and values, as well as Makeup elements (including unique abilities, accomplishments, and facts or statistics that offer proof of truth in advertising). Differentiation is the responsibility of a brand manager. Managing a personal brand also involves differentiating yourself from others in your field. The narrative of your story presented in the summary is a place to communicate differentiation that reveals how you specifically can create value for others.

- *Use multimedia to complement the written word*—Many LinkedIn profiles do not take advantage of the ability to add photos, videos, or documents that add to information communicated in text form. This tactic adds depth (or proof) to your written words and can lead to increased exposure for your content.[5]

Adopt a mindset that the summary section is not merely a box in the LinkedIn profile to fill in with basic descriptive text about your background, but rather is an invitation and outlet to tell your personal brand story.

Experience. When it comes to summarizing your work-related experience in your LinkedIn profile, you may feel completing this section is a breeze compared to writing a summary that thoroughly yet succinctly describes the value of your brand. All you have to do is list your current and previous jobs, your title, and duties performed, right? Wrong! Remember that your profile is like a marketing brochure for your brand; you must present your experience in a way that communicates the value you have to offer in a highly compelling way!

Career coach Melissa Llarena offers an alternative to the temptation to copy and paste experience information from your résumé in this crucial LinkedIn space. Her approach is based on the acronym PARS, which stands for:

- P—What is a *problem* you addressed?
- A—What are *actions* that you took to address the problem?
- R—What were the *results*?
- S—What *skills* did you develop or use to help achieve the results?[6]

If nothing else, you will likely differentiate yourself through presenting your experiences in this way, since most people stick to a straightforward description of title and duties (if they even do that much). You will tell a more complete story by adopting the PARS approach.

The experience section offers another opportunity to integrate multimedia content to provide evidence of your broad Makeup. Liberally use PowerPoint or SlideShare presentations, infographics, or video here.

Additionally, use keywords that will help you "turn up" more frequently in search results. For example, if your field is physical therapy, using words and terms related to physical therapy will boost your profile due to the large number of people routinely conducting searches for words like, for example, "physical therapy" or "physical therapist."

Last, if you are worried that your experience section may be lacking (or even if it is not), be sure to list volunteer experiences with nonprofit organizations in which you have participated. This information is a valuable way to demonstrate how you link your abilities (Makeup) to personal values (Meaning).

Honors and Awards. Including a description of recognition, honors, or awards received is a way for you to provide external validation of your abilities. Don't be shy! These forms of notoriety are important because they are bestowed on you by others to acknowledge your abilities. Awards are a form of social currency or validated proof that you offer value to others.

Some forms of recognition are formal, such as being named to the Dean's List or receiving a scholarship for academic achievement. Other forms of recognition are less formal, but should nonetheless be included to build the case for your brand value.

Melonie Dodaro, a social media strategist based in Kelowna, British Columbia, includes in the Honors and Awards section of her profile that she is widely recognized as Canada's #1 LinkedIn expert. Also, Dodaro lists media contributions (quotes in newspaper and magazine articles, as well as radio interviews) because being tapped to share your expertise with a media outlet's audience well represents a form of recognition.[7]

Skills and Endorsements. This section of the profile allows you to identify specific abilities or skills you possess. If you are new to LinkedIn, start by identifying ten skills you believe are the most relevant in your brand Makeup. You can list up to fifty skills, but be sure to prioritize skills that represent your greatest strengths and/or those that would be valued highly by others in the profession you work in or are targeting.

Be sure to take advantage of the opportunity to order the skills you list, creating a sort of ranking of your top skills. Listing the skills that are part of your brand Makeup will benefit you since others with similar skills will use this information to decide whether or not they think they would benefit by connecting with you. Another payoff of listing skills is that prospective employers can then use this section as an initial check point for a potential fit between you and their organization when an opportunity arises.

Another reason you want to create a skills list that reflects your greatest strengths is that your LinkedIn connections can provide validation of your skills using the Endorsements feature. Connections can endorse you for a given skill by going to your profile, clicking "Endorse," and selecting the skill or skills for which they wish to endorse you. If you are uncomfortable with receiving an endorsement for a particular skill, you are not obligated to keep the endorsement on your profile. If you ever happen to get endorsed for a skill for which you feel you are not worthy of an endorsement or otherwise do not want it to appear on your profile, the choice is yours to leave it there or not.

You are also not required to endorse connections in order to receive endorsements. However, it is good practice to reciprocate when appropriate. Practice the "give to get" approach to endorsements. Give them in recognition of the value you see in others and you are likely to get endorsements in return.

If there is a downside to endorsements, it is that they tend not to carry great weight with recruiters and hiring managers. The reason is simple— there is simply not much investment required on the part of the endorser to make a click with no burden of further explanation or reasoning given for the endorsement.

With that said, the number of endorsements you receive has a similar effect to the number of connections you have on LinkedIn. Both are social proof indicators that send a signal about the quality and reach of your personal brand.

Recommendations. Endorsements can be a nice addition to your profile. However, you will want to utilize another profile feature to gain stronger support from connections to make a case for your brand value: recommendations.

At some point in the past, you may have asked someone to write a letter of recommendation for you in order to be considered for a job, college admission, or an award. Think of LinkedIn recommendations as permanent letters; they remain on your profile as long as you want them there.

How important are recommendations to building credibility for your brand? Employment recruiters have differing views, with some recruiters saying you should have ten or more recommendations. Other recruiters say the number of recommendations is not as important as the quality of a recommendation. General statements such as "Erin is a hard worker," for instance, does not have the same impact as a brief story or example that specifically illustrates Erin's tireless work ethic in a time crunch.

LinkedIn recommendations are no different from traditional letters of recommendation in that some writers put more thought and effort into writing a recommendation than others do. So who do you ask to write recommendations for you? Begin by only asking first-degree connections (people with whom you are connected already on LinkedIn). Also, do not ask family or friends to write recommendation letters unless you have worked with them and they can speak to your professional capabilities. The same prospects for writing a traditional recommendation letter are the same people who can write a LinkedIn recommendation on your behalf, namely former professors, supervisors, customers, and vendors frequently approached to make recommendations.

Asking for a recommendation on LinkedIn is rather simple. On the Recommendations section of your profile, simply click "Ask to be recommended." You can ask for and make recommendations from this section.

One very important point to remember about asking for a recommendation is this: Do not use LinkedIn's default statement for requesting a recommendation. It reads: *"I'm writing to ask if you would write a brief recommendation of my work that I can include on my LinkedIn profile. If you have any questions, please let me know. Thanks in advance for your help."*

If you use the default request, you will likely come across to the recipient of your request as lazy and insincere. Take a few moments to personalize your request by writing your own statement personalized to the recipient and tailor your request to guide the writer on exactly what you wish for them to include in the recommendation (such as asking a professor to comment on your performance in group projects).

Publishing

Your profile is the most important marketing asset for brand building on LinkedIn. Another promotional tool is relatively new: LinkedIn Pulse, a blog-like content creation feature.

Unlike a blog dependent on the promotional efforts of the blogger and word-of-mouth from readers to build audience, LinkedIn Pulse provides you a built-in audience of LinkedIn users. Your connections will automatically see any posts you make on Pulse, and good content is often shared with their connections. Essentially, a typical LinkedIn user enjoys greater reach right off the bat than does a personal blog.

The content of a Pulse post is similar to a traditional blog post. It could be expressing your viewpoint on a topic or trend in your field, writing a synopsis of a current event, or demonstrating expertise by writing about research you have conducted. Posting your work on Pulse is simple—just click on the pencil icon in the "Share an update" box at the top of the LinkedIn home page to create a post.

LinkedIn expert Viveka Von Rosen has shared several helpful hints about what has made her Pulse posts effective:

- A catchy title.
- An attractive image that fits the topical focus of the post (or video).
- Post lengths of 300-600 words.
- Using keywords that make posts easier to find by the audience you most wish to attract.
- Sharing a link to your post through other social media channels.

In addition to the above tactics that are within your control, Von Rosen points out one other ingredient for success that isn't: luck.[8] While it's true that not every post will be a home run in terms of the number of likes and shares, keep in mind that home runs are not necessarily the reason to post in the first place (although they are a nice boost every once in a while!). Writing a post that you think would be of interest to your professional network on LinkedIn is a way that you give your talents and abilities to create value for others. Wider exposure for your personal brand is a positive by-product of the writing process.

Networking

Once you have completed your profile and begin to test the waters of publishing using Pulse, turn your attention to LinkedIn's most potent benefit: networking opportunities with people around the world who have similar interests as you do.

Whether you are new to LinkedIn or have been a user for some time, the thought of making connections with strangers can be intimidating. This feeling might be especially poignant when you are a student or in the beginning stages of your career. You may feel like you don't have much to offer, or question why someone would want to connect with you given your relative lack of experience. Keep in mind that the purpose of networking is to build relationships that have the *potential* to benefit both parties. Great things don't have to happen today for a connection made on LinkedIn to be a worthwhile investment made. If you operate with this mindset, you will find networking on LinkedIn less daunting.

Three ways to use LinkedIn for networking include connecting with individual users, joining LinkedIn groups, and following companies.

Connect with Individuals

Now that you are in the connections game, using proper "connection etiquette" can be the difference between your request being accepted or declined by the recipient.

The low hanging fruit of your LinkedIn professional network is people you know already, a.k.a. your friends, relatives, neighbors, classmates, and co-workers. These are the people in your "real life" network that should be part of your LinkedIn network, too.

When you connect with someone, he or she becomes a first-degree connection. Connections you make stemming from your first-degree connections are second-degree connections. Rest assured, you will find second-degree connections with whom you would like to connect. Utilize your network by asking your first-degree connection if he or she is willing to make an introduction on your behalf. Be sure to let your connection know why you would like to meet his or her connection in the first place. An introduction from a mutual connection usually includes some information about you for the person you want to meet, giving that person a better understanding of why you have a desire to connect.

One important piece of connection etiquette is to send connection requests only to people you know in some way. When making a connection request, LinkedIn asks how you know the person. Are you a colleague, classmate, business associate, or friend? If you do not the person in any of these ways, it is advisable not to send a connection request at all.

One of the biggest mistakes you can make networking on LinkedIn is to use the default connection request. It reads *"I would like to add you to my professional network on LinkedIn."* Even when you are requesting to connect with some you know already, this message comes across as very impersonal. Others will recognize it as the connection template and see your request as a lazy attempt to connect.

The most important practice when it comes to making a proper connection request is to tailor your message specifically to the person with whom you wish to connect. You would not have the same conversation with every person you meet when talking face-to-face. Similarly, your online communication should not be based on a template that a website provides.

Elements to include in a LinkedIn connection request include:

- Introduction of who you are, including your title or role, and your mutual connection.

- Explanation of how you found the person (it could be from conducting a LinkedIn search, or you may belong to one or more of the same LinkedIn groups, or are a reader of the person's blog, or are aware of the person's expertise or accomplishments in his or her field. This is key because the person receiving the request will be curious how you found him or her).

- Justify why you want to connect with the person. The *"I want to add you to my professional network…"* statement that is the default connection request is not justification! Give the other person a reason to want to connect with you! Perhaps you are an admirer of his or her professional work, or you can always remark that you have friends or colleagues in common. Tell them!

Understand that not all of your connection requests will be accepted even when you follow proper connection etiquette. Do not take it personally, as people differ in their approaches to how to build their LinkedIn network. For instance, some members want as large of a network as possible and are very open to networking with people they do not know. Other people confine their LinkedIn network to people they know offline.

Become Active in Groups

Whether you are new to LinkedIn or have been a member for some time, an often underutilized source for extending your professional network is the Groups feature.

LinkedIn Groups form around particular interests, industry or professional organizations, alumni of a college, or former employees of a company. For example, a chemical engineer could belong to The Chemical Engineer (shared interest), AIChE (American Institute of Chemical Engineers), and/or U.S. Army Engineers Alumni (current and former Army Engineers group). A search of chemical engineer returns more than 70 groups. (You can belong to up to 50 groups on LinkedIn.) Differing opinions exist about whether you should join as many groups as possible to broaden your network or focus on a small number of groups and be very active with them. Both views have positive points. You can follow either approach. The main point is to take advantage of LinkedIn Groups.

Why exactly should you join groups on LinkedIn? A typical group includes discussions of topics that relate to members' interests, promotes useful content, and posts jobs. Members use Groups to ask questions to learn more or to solve a problem, seek advice on how to handle specific job situations, or stimulate conversation about topics or trends affecting group members. Some groups have open membership, meaning all you have to do is click "Join" and you are in. Other groups are closed and require that a group administrator approve your request to join. Some groups are plagued by a small number of members that post sales-related messages frequently that come across more like spam than the useful content you expect from a LinkedIn group. Proactive group administrators police this behavior and strive to keep it out of their groups.

Being active in LinkedIn groups benefits you in three ways:

Learning. Reading discussions posted by group members gives you perspectives that can add to your knowledge of your field. The experiences of members are valuable in their own development and you can benefit from the knowledge, successes, and failures they experienced and now share.

Prospecting. Following discussions and other posts on a LinkedIn group can be beneficial in identifying individuals that stand out as thought leaders. These people demonstrate expertise, insight, and understanding that make them influential among their peers. Connecting with thought leaders in your field can be less daunting if you begin building a relationship with them through group interactions.

Networking. Last but not least, use Groups to add connections to your network. When you have group membership in common with someone else, it serves as a filter for identifying potential additions to your network and is common ground upon which you can make a connection request. An example of this benefit could play out like this using a scenario of a college student studying information technology reaching out to a professional for a connection: *"Mr. Wilson, I have been reading your posts on the IT Architect Network for several weeks and have enjoyed reading your thoughts about current trends in our field. As someone about to begin her career in IT, I would value the chance to be connected with you professionally."* This example serves as a reminder to ditch the connection request template provided by LinkedIn and to tailor your message to show the recipient why you are asking to connect.

Finally, while there are about two million different LinkedIn groups, it is still possible that you might not find one that serves a certain niche or interest that you have. The good news is if a group does not exist, someone can start it… and that someone could be you!

Follow Companies

A third way to use LinkedIn to build your professional network is to follow companies, and you can follow up to 10,000 different companies.

Unlike a connection request that requires the other party to reciprocate in order to make a connection, following a company is done simply by clicking the "Follow" button. Immediately, you will begin to see updates from the company on your LinkedIn page. Although you are not directly interacting with a company, you can then follow it in the same way you do with an individual with whom you are connected.

Career coach Miriam Salpeter has pointed out several benefits of following companies:

- *It is a way to learn about developments within a company* – such as a new venture, product launch, market expansion, or other news that could offer opportunities for you.

- *It serves as a research function* – LinkedIn will suggest companies for you to follow based on companies you follow currently, thus pointing out other firms that could be of interest to you but of which you may currently be unaware.

- *You learn from others* – Check out the profile page of your connections to see what companies they follow. Their lists likely include companies with which you are unfamiliar or would not have thought to seek out on LinkedIn.

- *It signals your interest in an organization* – Following a company is a form of endorsement and can be interpreted as you having an interest in that company. Remember that LinkedIn is a two-way street; it is not just job seekers looking for employment. Recruiters are actively looking for new talent to bring into their organization. Setting up a company profile page is absolutely used by employers to "pull" interested people to the brand.[9]

Learning

So far, we have covered how to use LinkedIn for promotion and online communications with other LinkedIn members (elements of brand Message), and building a professional network of connections (a part of brand Makeup). A third benefit of LinkedIn for marketing your personal brand is that it is an excellent resource for learning, which is another aspect of brand Makeup.

With LinkedIn, you have at your fingertips a collection of professionals from your field (as well as others) from which you can gain tips, ideas, and perspective. Three specific uses of LinkedIn for learning include optimizing your Updates Feed, listening and participating in group discussions, and discovering job opportunities.

Updates Feed

Logging in on LinkedIn takes you to your home page. The user experience of the updates feed resembles that of Facebook. You will see status updates from people and companies that you follow. Like Facebook, you can interact with others' status updates by liking, commenting, or sharing. Also, LinkedIn will recommend content from Pulse that it believes could be of interest to you.

The updates feed is an ideal starting point when you first log in as it allows you to catch up on what is going on with people in your network (birthdays, promotions, new jobs, new connections), stay current with news and trends in your interest areas, and identify prospective connections to your LinkedIn network.

Your updates feed will give you a taste of the content available on Pulse, but dive deeper into Pulse to check out articles and information being posted on LinkedIn that match your interests. Access Pulse from the Interests tab on the home page. Once there, you will find suggestions for content to follow organized by author (influencers such as Richard Branson, Bill Gates, and Guy Kawasaki), channel (topics such as technology, entrepreneurship, and healthcare), and publisher (traditional publishers such as *The Wall Street Journal*, *Harvard Business Review*, and *Time*, all of which use Pulse). Make Pulse a part of your learning and continuous improvement efforts to strengthen brand Makeup.

Group Discussions

Joining LinkedIn groups is not only an effective tactic for growing your network of professional contacts but is also a great learning source.

The discussions that take place in a group are initiated by members. Like any post on a social networking site, some posts elicit many responses, while others trigger no interaction whatsoever. The topics of posts made in a group can be wide ranging. For example, discussion posts to the group Social Media Marketing might include links to articles, blogs, infographics, and/or discussions that begin with a question such as "what types of content perform best on social media" or "what advice can you give a graduating student looking to start a career in social media marketing," and/or promotional posts for one's own company or services. Being a regular visitor to your LinkedIn groups enables you to stay informed on what people in your profession are talking about and thinking about and to stay abreast of the problems or challenges that they (and you!) face.

The benefit of participating in LinkedIn groups increases when members not only read discussions but contribute by commenting, sharing, and liking posts. At the same time, being active in a LinkedIn group is a way to identify people you would want to network with beyond just being members of the same group. LinkedIn lets you "follow" group members, enabling you to see their discussion posts when you click on the group. If you find the posts of certain group members to be consistently informative or useful, following those members lets you keep up with their posts conveniently. And, of course, it also strengthens your link to them.

Discovering Jobs

Last but certainly not least, LinkedIn is a channel for finding a job. Too many people mistake this characteristic of LinkedIn as its main reason for existence. First and foremost, as exhibited throughout this chapter, LinkedIn is an online community.

That said, one way members of a community help one another is to create awareness of opportunities. You can use LinkedIn to learn what types of jobs are in demand, which companies are hiring, and the geographic areas where opportunities exist. Specifically, you should tap into four different LinkedIn features to aid in a job search: the jobs tab, the group jobs tab, company pages, and your news feed.

Jobs tab. One of the tabs at the top of the LinkedIn home page is "Jobs." The search capabilities enable you to filter search results by keyword, job title, and location (country, zip code, and distance from a location). For example, a search using the keywords "registered dietician" using a zip code for the Miami, Florida area, returned ten jobs posted. In addition to doing a specific job search, you can use the Jobs feature to do a broad search to gain an understanding of the number of opportunities available and where the jobs are located. Also, information in the job postings can be valuable in learning more about the specific skills sought and experience expected for someone in that position.

Groups job tab. The Groups feature has been touted as beneficial to expanding your network and learning about an industry or topic from group members. A third benefit of maximizing groups on LinkedIn is access to information on available jobs. Group members could have open positions in their organizations or have received a job posting from someone in their network. Posting job opportunities is one way group members are able to help one another, and the person posting a job could be someone you want to connect with (if not connected already) to learn more about the job.

Company pages. Following companies has been discussed as a means of networking, while at the same time offering an opportunity to learn more about a certain organization and its employees that are active on LinkedIn. Keep in mind that one of the purposes of company pages is for marketing the organization to prospective employees. Follow company pages to learn more about current happenings, including information on available jobs.

Updates feed. Review your updates feed to check out new posts by connections in your network since newly available jobs are a common topic of those updates. If you are connected with recruiters or others in hiring roles in their companies, they will likely post updates about available jobs. Other connections in your network could share job opportunities as a favor to one of their connections who posts about a job, or to spread information they believe their connections would find valuable.

Take Action

Ask yourself these important questions and/or take the following actions before we proceed with the process of building your personal brand.

1. Review your LinkedIn profile, evaluating each of the eight sections discussed in this chapter using a 1-10 scale with 1 being

"unacceptable" and 10 being "exceptional." Which sections of your profile are strengths? Which sections need to be improved? What changes are needed to improve the weakest sections? Want a second opinion? Ask a connection to evaluate your profile in the same way and give you feedback.

2. Pick two LinkedIn groups on which you will focus attention for the next four weeks. Set weekly goals for engagement (number of likes and comments), participation, number of posts, and networking (the number of people you want to follow or request to connect). Then, repeat by identifying two more groups and again setting weekly goals for engagement, participation, and networking.

A League of Its Own

Your LinkedIn Profile should summarize who you are. You must communicate your value specifically and succinctly. So how will you write the story of you? Creating a list that reflects your key strengths and the value you bring to others is a great start.

What's Included in This Package

Your Greatest Strengths and Summary & Keywords Reports will help you identify your key strengths and keywords to describe you, enabling you to articulate "Brand You" on your LinkedIn Profile.

Take Action: Self-Assess NOW **http://bit.ly/SelfAssessME**

15.

CONTENT: THE FUEL OF BRAND MESSAGE

"Traditional marketing and advertising is telling the world you're a rock star.
Content marketing is showing the world that you are one."
—Robert Rose, content marketing strategist and author

The social media communication channels discussed in Chapters 13 and 14 play a vital role in delivering your brand Message. Those channels also share something else in common: they are other people's property.

You are merely borrowing space on LinkedIn, Facebook, or any other social networking site. Someone else owns the real estate, they set the rules, and they can also change the rules at any point they deem appropriate to best suit their agenda. That's because social networks are businesses, too! Several of the major ones are publicly owned and thus are accountable to stockholders to deliver profits.

An example of how this characteristic of social media can affect a brand's marketing efforts is Facebook's treatment of organic (unpaid) content posted by brands. Changes to Facebook's algorithm have dramatically reduced a given brand's ability to reach their communities with non-paid posts, with estimates of organic reach being in the range of three to six percent. This means that for every one-hundred Facebook users who like a brand page, approximately ninety-five of them will probably never see a given non-paid post made by a brand. The rationale for this shift is easy to understand—Facebook wants brands to pay to reach users just as they would pay to place ads in magazines or on television programs.

You may be wondering how the shift by social networks toward forcing more paid audience access affects your personal branding efforts. It has little effect if you are using social networking sites strictly for learning (other than maybe not being able to see all posts from brands that you like on Facebook). If you are using social networking sites as primary channel for extending the reach of your brand, however, you can see how relying on borrowed real estate to build your brand might be risky. The audience that you work so hard to build may not be as reachable as you think.

Fortunately, an alternative exists that overcomes obstacles imposed by social networking sites' algorithms or other policies that negatively affect organic audience reach. That alternative is content marketing, a strategy of proactively producing information and distributing it through your own digital channels. Although content marketing falls under your brand Message strategy, it is all about building a platform for expressing your brand Meaning and Makeup. This chapter explores channels for using content to connect your brand with people and organizations you seek to reach.

What is Content Marketing?

The availability of new communication channels has given individuals and brands a voice to express a viewpoint and share their expertise. You need more than channels to package and distribute messages, though. A strategy is needed that sets communication objectives, the types of information you can produce that will be valuable others, and a distribution plan that includes how messages will be delivered (channels), as well as timetables for content delivery. That's why content marketing is a "must-have" piece of your brand Message.

If the term content marketing is new to you, let's demystify what it is and why it's relevant. Content marketing is a process of attracting and retaining an audience through content creation and curation with the goal of influencing behavior.[1] This definition has three key dimensions:

- *Process*—Content marketing requires planning to determine why you should be a content distributor, what content to communicate, and the best way to deliver it to your target audience. It requires an ongoing commitment to implementing the why, what, and how of content marketing. Being a content marketer is not a "one and done" campaign or a short-term effort. Like personal branding, once you crank up your content marketing machine, be prepared to tend to it forever.

- *Created or curated*—If the thought of producing original content through writing, video, or audio is overwhelming to you, the good news is that content marketing is not solely about creating content yourself. You can also focus on collecting and sharing information you believe your audience will find useful. This content curation helps to filter the vast amount of information on the Internet. You add value by performing the task of finding and sharing articles, blog posts, videos, and other forms of content you think others will find interesting or relevant.

- *Influencing behavior*—Clearly identify outcomes you expect to achieve with a content marketing strategy. You may have broad objectives such as expanding the size of your professional network or developing a brand reputation for expertise. Or, you may have more specific objectives like connecting with leaders in your field or attracting interest from a prospective employer. Starting with goals in mind will give direction to the "what" of content creation/curation and "how" of content distribution.

Interest in content marketing may be new, but it is a concept rooted in "old school" marketing. In a nutshell, content marketing is about how you can use information (content) to be a useful resource to other people. Or, as marketing expert and author Jay Baer puts it, "youtility." Content that offers utility or benefit to others elevates your reputation by building trust among the people you reach.

How Content Marketing Helps Your Brand

Content marketing has become a communication staple for most organizations. Research by the Content Marketing Institute found that 83% of business-to-business (B2B) firms and 77% of business-to-consumer (B2C) firms have a content marketing strategy in place.[2]

The benefits of content marketing are not limited to B2B and B2C brands. Personal brands can also use a content marketing strategy to stand out and create a distinctive brand position.

Personal branding expert Jill Celeste says there are six reasons why content marketing should be a part of your personal brand building plan:

- *Demonstrate expertise*—Content you create lets you "show what you know," building brand credibility.
- *Build authority*—As your credibility rises, you can be perceived as a valued resource in your industry or niche.

- *Gain trust*—Posting credible, quality content influences perceptions of trustworthiness among people who have never met you. Their use of your content begins to serve as an indicator of the level of trust they and others should put in your brand.

- *Get found online*—Content creation is a huge plus for search engine optimization (SEO) for your brand. You will be much easier to find online in Google searches and the like when you consistently create and post content.

- *Build a following*—Your efforts to create and curate content will lead others to you, expanding your professional network. One big payoff to optimizing your online presence by posting content is that it makes it easier for people to find you.

- *Continuous learning*—Creating or sharing great content is the output of learning and personal development. Committing to managing your brand Message through content marketing is also a decision to commit to ongoing learning and growth in your field.[3]

Like any other aspect of marketing, there are many examples of bad content marketing practices to be found. Dabbling in content marketing because "everyone else is doing it" is not a strategy. Consider which of the six benefits of using content to build your personal brand are most important to your success, then let your decisions about which content channels you will use be guided by what exactly you wish to accomplish.

Content Channels

A key to using content marketing to realize the benefits of expertise, authority, trust, and exposure is choosing channels to distribute content where you can find the people you want to reach. Your messaging can be outstanding, but if it does not get to the audience that would find it valuable, your efforts may be in vain.

Numerous options exist as potential channels for a personal brand content marketing strategy. However, four channels stand out because of their popularity and impact. They are blogs, video, podcasts, and social media.

Blogs

The term blog is shorthand for "weblog." A popular positioning for early blogs of the late 1990s and early 2000s was an online diary.

While blogs still serve this role, they have evolved into an important self-publishing platform for both product and personal brands. The availability of user-friendly blog publishing services such as Blogger and WordPress have made it possible for anyone with an Internet connection and keyboard to become a content publisher. Witness the fact that more than 200 million blogs exist today on virtually every topic imaginable, including hobbies, news, personal journeys, and much more.

Although most blogs are published by individuals, many businesses have jumped on the blog bandwagon and started publishing content for their customers and prospects. Research done by the Content Marketing Institute found that 80% of B2B firms and 67% of B2C firms use blogs as part of their content marketing strategy.[4]

The benefits of blogging are not limited to corporate and product brands. A blog is vital for building a personal brand. Managing one's personal brand shares similarities with product branding in that both are practiced through developing a differentiated offering and communicating it to a clearly defined audience.[5]

One widely held view of the benefits of blogging for a personal brand is the impact on thought leadership. Thought leadership recognition *as a foremost authority in selected areas of specialization and profiting significantly from fulfilling that role.*[6] Individuals can demonstrate expertise through content published on their blogs and exert influence over their readership when readers like, share, or comment.

In addition to articulating knowledge that can build one's standing as a thought leader, a blog can impact readers on an emotional level when an author shares stories that have shaped his or her personal brand. Although you will never meet most of the people who might read your blog, they will feel a connection with you if they can relate to the thoughts, stories, and struggles shared in your posts. The payoff of blogging can be to differentiate your personal brand amid the sea of all those self-proclaimed "experts" and "gurus" (remember them?). Blogging is an opportunity to craft a brand voice and message that communicates unique value and reflects your personality.

Finding Your Blogging Style

The benefits of blogging are well documented, but taking the plunge and becoming a blogger can be understandably very intimidating. You might ask yourself "who would bother reading my blog posts" or "what could I write about on a regular basis?"

The latter question is the more important one—don't get too concerned with audience size until you establish a pattern of writing that would attract people in the first place. Many bloggers (including us, the authors of this book!) wrestle with these thoughts. You are far from being alone.

Blogging experts Mark Schaefer and Stanford Smith (authors of *Born to Blog*) studied more than 500 blogs to identify certain traits or skills exhibited by blog authors. Their findings suggest five different blogging styles, or voices that can be used to position yourself and your blog: dreamer, storyteller, persuader, teacher, and curator.[7]

Dreamer. Bloggers who are dreamers are able to describe the world as they see it, whether it be reality or just possibilities. Just as dreams or visions of what might be can serve as the inspiration for a new business or product, so too can they stir a person's creativity for writing blog posts. One of the most popular bloggers who oftentimes writes in this style is the aforementioned marketing expert Seth Godin, who posts daily about his visions of how companies and individuals should aspire for greatness.

Storyteller. Earlier in the book the expression "facts tell but stories sell" was referenced. Stories bring thoughts and ideas to life, making them interesting and entertaining. An element of many stories is emotion. You can open up and show the "real you" by sharing your feelings and writing about topics that matter, either professionally or personally. A storytelling style is a good fit for blog posts about life experiences and emotions, such as the ups and downs of searching for your first job out of college or dealing with being laid off from a job.

Persuader. This blogging style involves using your writing to influence the thoughts and opinions of others. Schaefer and Smith say keys to this style include building trust and strengthening relationships. It is not necessarily the words you write that make you persuasive but rather the value placed on the words by readers. Schaefer and Smith cite the impact blogs had on Barack Obama's rise from relative obscurity to overtake Democratic frontrunner Hillary Clinton in 2008 on his way to two terms as President of the United States. Obama's blog posts built his credibility and helped position him as an attractive alternative candidate.

Teacher. If you enjoy helping other people or solving problems, adopting a teaching style could make blogging a satisfying and successful endeavor. Posts that teach people something provide readers a direct benefit, enabling them to know or do something they did not know or could not do before reading your blog. You can write posts that inform, inspire action, or coach readers through a situation. An example of a teaching-style blog is one written by James Wedmore, a video marketing expert. Many of Wedmore's posts help readers better understand different aspects of creating and using video. A teaching style is not limited to technical or complex situations; anything that requires learning could be fair game as blog material.

Curator. The first four blogging styles share a common characteristic in that each subsists on the creation and writing of original content. Curation, by contrast, involves sifting through vast amount of content already on the Internet (articles, videos, blog posts, etc.) and compiling what you believe to be the most relevant, relatable works that you think people would find valuable. Acting as a curator is a way to attract an audience of people who have similar interests. For example, marketing expert Mitch Joel has a weekly-themed post titled "Six Links Worthy of Your Attention." Each post is a collection of six articles or videos Joel, along with two friends, found interesting and which they share with other (and Joel's blog audience). Curation is a way for beginning bloggers to come up with ideas for posts without having to create original content.

You may be wondering at this point which blogging style you should adopt. Keep two points in mind about these styles. First, you are not obliged to choose one and only one. Joel's writing on his Six Pixels of Separation blog is, for instance, varied. If you read a number of his posts, you will come to the conclusion that he has written in each of the five styles. Second, you will achieve the best results when adopting a blogging style that fits your personality. Are you opinionated? Or do you like telling

203

stories? Have a knack for explaining things? Follow your muse! After all, you want your blog to express your authentic personal brand!

Blog Options

Your blog is a crucial piece of real estate for communicating brand Message. Thus, the decision as to where to house your blog is important for making your content marketing strategy a success.

Two general options are available for choosing a site to host your blog: 1.) a blog website, or 2.) a self-hosted blog.

Blog Website. If you are new to blogging or do not have funds to budget for a domain name and a blog hosting service, setting up a blog on a blogging website is a no-cost way to quickly (and affordably!) get in the blogging game. A blog can be set up for free on sites such as Blogger, WordPress.com, and Tumblr, removing any financial barriers to blogging. The no-cost characteristic of these sites is the primary advantage of using them. Another advantage of free blog websites is that their web presence or domain serves as a portal, or point of entry, in which readers enter to look for blogs of interest to them. A third advantage of free blog websites is that they are easy to set up and maintain. Free templates are provided from which you can select how your blog will look. Heavy-duty code writing is not necessary, as the work to create blog architecture has already been done for you.

Using a free blog website for your blog home has two drawbacks, though, that you must take into consideration. First, the default domain for your blog will be that of the blog website, not a distinctive identity you can create. For example, if you choose Blogger to host your blog about Millennials and financial management, your URL might be something like http://millennialsandmoney.blogspot.com. This characteristic of free blogs can be more of a drawback if it is important for you to project your individual brand identity.

It is possible to direct visitors to a Blogger or Tumblr blog to a custom domain that you can purchase from GoDaddy or another domain name registrar. The cost to have a custom domain could be as little as around $10 per year depending on the availability and demand for the domain name you want.

A second drawback associated with free blog website services is that they offer fewer creative options for blog design compared to the availability of designs or themes for self-hosted blogs. Free design templates are suitable enough for many new and even established bloggers. However, if the visual appeal of your blog is crucial to your brand position, it is possible that templates provided by free blog websites will not meet your needs. For example, if you are a photographer or artist with a need to create a strong visual presence, you may prefer to have a custom blog template designed that better enables you to show off your works and express your personal brand.

Self-Hosted Blog. Launching a blog on a free blog website overcomes two obstacles that keep many would-be bloggers from getting started: limited financial resources and lack of technical skills. You can begin blogging on a free blog website and move to a self-hosted blog as your confidence as a blogger and need for a more impressive marketing presence grow.

A self-hosted blog is one that is located on a service on which a blogger pays for a web hosting account. Two costs that you will incur with a self-hosted blog are domain name purchase and web hosting fees. Both costs are typically paid annually. The most popular self-hosted blog uses the WordPress.org platform. Bloggers are drawn to the wide variety of themes or designs available here, either free or paid, as well as the availability of applications known as plug-ins that add features to a blog (such as social sharing buttons, comments, e-commerce functions, and more).

The benefits of a self-hosted blog essentially play off the drawbacks of using a free blog service. The main benefit is the increased latitude for branding your blog. Your domain name can be selected specifically to reference your name, company brand, or blog subject matter. If you have your own domain name, you will not have the name of the blog service attached to it—you will only have the identity you wish to create.

Another benefit of a self-hosted blog is the greater creative flexibility inherent to your blog's layout and functionality. You will have more themes to choose from (free or paid), and you can add whatever plug-ins you desire to create a heightened user experience for your blog visitors.

Each option for your blog home has advantages and disadvantages. Weigh the attributes of each blog type against your Message goals and content strategy to determine which one is best for you. Also, keep in mind that your decision is not necessarily permanent. If you opt for a free blog on Blogger or WordPress.com, you can import that content if you decide later to switch to a self-hosted WordPress.org blog.

Video

Blogging is a valuable content marketing channel as it can amplify your voice and viewpoint. That said, it is not the ideal channel to reach everyone who might be interested in connecting with you.

Video is another communication channel for publishing and can also complement your blogging efforts. The decision to produce video content does not however have to be specifically to complement your blogging efforts. You can incorporate video into blogs, use video as a channel to send stand-alone messages, or you can even use video as your blog. An example is Amy Schmittauer's Savvy Sexy Social blog. Schmittauer blogs about social media and content marketing, and her posts are produced in video form rather than a text-based format usually associated with a blog.

If the thought of getting in front of a camera terrifies you, consider the impact video has on audience engagement:

- Online video reaches 60 % of the U.S. population.
- Retention of information consumed via video can be as high as 65% compared to around 10% for text information.
- 65% of video watchers view 75% or more of a video.
- 74% of all Internet traffic will be video by 2017.[8]

These statistics offer compelling reasons to overcome your fears and consider how you might use video as part of your content marketing strategy.

Video can also boost the quality of your content through the addition of a visual and audio communication channel. Viewers not only process your message in words, but imagery projected on video creates associations with your personality.

Using the blog example above, Schmittauer the person is on display in her blog as much as Schmittauer the marketing professional. Human nature leads us to be attracted to people who we like, trust, and perceive to have similarity. Video gives people the next best thing to interacting with you in person.

Luckily, equipment needs for producing video have become quite affordable. In fact, the high-definition camera on a smartphone is all you really need to at least get started creating video content for your blog. You certainly do not need a video production crew and high-dollar gear. More importantly, you need to acknowledge the value video can bring to your blog and takes steps to add this value for others by providing video content.

Podcasts

A third channel for producing content to share with audiences in your profession or industry is podcasts. A podcast is a digital audio file that can be downloaded from the Internet and listened to on a computer, tablet, smartphone, or portable audio player.

A podcast is a cross between a blog and talk radio show. Podcast content formats vary from interviews, question and answer sessions, panel discussions, and one-way broadcasting. The format a podcaster adopts should be driven by the needs and wants of their target audience.

For example, career expert Dan Miller hosts a weekly career strategies podcast called 48 Days. The content of each podcast is driven primarily by questions submitted by listeners that Miller answers on air. Other podcasts discuss current events or are built around interviewing experts in a field related to the podcast's topical focus.

Podcasting was presumed dead just a few years ago but is currently enjoying a resurgence as the ease of downloading or streaming podcasts makes consumption easier than ever before. It's estimated that the number of unique podcast listeners tripled from twenty-five million to seventy-five million in 2013.[9]

An example of a podcaster who has benefited from this rapid growth is Jeff Sanders. In 2011, Sanders launched his "The 5 AM Miracle" podcast. He ventured into podcasting after successfully blogging for two years. His podcast quickly rose to the top of the charts for business podcasts on iTunes. He cites five benefits of podcasting:

- *Expand your network*—Sanders has met several celebrities and well-known experts by inviting them to be interviewed for his podcast.

- *Reach a whole new audience base*—Podcast listeners can be a separate audience from people reached through the blogging platform.

- *Strengthen networking*—The trust and credibility built through podcasting led to new business opportunities for Sanders.

- *Practice public speaking skills*—You do not have to be a DJ or professional speaker to get into podcasting. You will no doubt sharpen speaking skills, though, through the process of creating, producing, and distributing podcasts.

- *Become more personal*—A podcast lets your personality come through in ways not possible through a blog.[10]

You may have no desire to have a top-ranked podcast, but you must recognize the value podcasting can create for you and the audience you seek to reach even as just a small part of your personal brand building effort.

If you decide to make podcasts part of your content marketing strategy, you will face the same decision that bloggers face: Where should your podcast be hosted? Similar to blog hosting, you have two general options for podcast hosting. One option is to utilize free hosting services such as BlogTalkRadio or SoundCloud. These websites attract listeners due to the wide variety of content available on their base platform. The second option is to use a hosting service. The file sizes of podcasts can be quite large, so selecting a service that accommodates the needs of podcasting is important. Amazon S3, Blubrry, and Libsyn are popular hosting services commonly used by podcasters.

A podcast is no different from any other communication tactic in that you are not obligated to use it forever. Podcasts may be an ideal medium for reaching an audience to spread your message at one point in time, but as your career evolves, it may no longer be such a good fit for your evolving brand Message strategy.

For example, Patrick Schwerdtfeger, a real estate professional, launched a podcast called "Beyond the Note" in 2006. The focus of his podcast was educating people on the mortgage application process and answering questions from his audience. The podcast grew to over seventy-five thousand downloads in twenty-seven countries. "Beyond the Note" ran its course, though, and Schwerdtfeger no longer produces the podcast. Why? The professional growth and new business opportunities that arose from people impacted by his podcast led to Schwerdtfeger choosing to reposition his brand as a professional speaker instead.[11]

Social Media

A final channel for publishing content is one we examined in Chapters 13 and 14: social networking websites.

When you share updates, blog posts, photos, or videos to Facebook, Twitter, Instagram, Pinterest, Google+, or LinkedIn, you are engaging in a form of content marketing. Recall that the main difference between the content channels discussed in this chapter (blogs, video, and podcasts) and social media is ownership of the real estate where the content is published. Content classified as owned media (channels that you control, such as your website and blog) is housed in places you control. Social networking websites, by contrast, are the equivalent of rented spaces. Although the rent is free, the landlords set the rules for content distribution (and the rules are being increasingly being revised in the favor of the social networking sites). Most notably, reach of posts on some social networking websites is enhanced when one opts to buy paid placement or advertising.

Never forget that the social networks are businesses. They set the ground rules in ways that benefit them. Thus, product and personal brands must always be thinking about how to make the most of the opportunities afforded on social networking sites to complement their owned media strategy.

Three tactics you can employ to utilize earned media (exposure created by social sharing) to push content to target audiences are video, hashtags, and engagement.

Video. Recall the statistics shared earlier in this chapter about video's retention rate and audience engagement. It is clearly a powerful channel for capturing and keeping attention. Video is the most valued content form on Facebook. Specifically, video posted to Facebook and not shared from YouTube or another website tends to have greater organic (unpaid) reach. Why? Facebook knows that video is compelling content that will likely keep users on the site longer. As such, consider how you might use videos on Facebook to extend your message reach and attract an audience. A weekly update, recaps of conferences attended, and interviews of professionals in your field are three examples of the many possibilities available for using video on Facebook. Twitter and Instagram are other social networking sites that offer the option of posting video, although the videos must be relatively short, with a maximum length of 30 seconds and 15 seconds, respectively.

Hashtags. The abundance of content being published today is like a fire hose of information. Readers are being doused with a constant stream of posts, articles, podcasts, and more from corporate brands and individuals alike. You can easily become overwhelmed by the amount of content that is available for consumption and end up missing out on content that would actually be valuable to you! Similarly, how do you direct your valuable content toward the people who would be most interested in it without just being part of the deluge? After all, they are being sprayed with the same information firehose as you are!

One solution to creating targeted content is to make use of hashtags as you post across different channels. The use of hashtags gained popularity among Twitter users but has spread to Facebook, Instagram, Pinterest, Google+, and Tumblr. If you are a social media user, you likely already use hashtags to give context to messages that you send, as well as signal others which messages you find interesting. Hashtags are used to participate in discussions about major events such as when the President of the United States makes the State of the Union address (#SOTU) or during the NCAA basketball tournament (#MarchMadness). Content related to your professional interests can be found in the same manner. Examples of content organized around professional topics include #leadership and #SQL (a programming language for database management).

If you find the use of hashtags confusing or even annoying, reconsider your opinion of hashtags and look for opportunities to tag your content to make it easier for your target audience to find it. Hashtags offer two valuable benefits for personal branding. First, hashtags have the functional benefit of organizing and targeting your posts, videos, or other content. It signals to others the subject or topic of your content, serving as a filter or checkpoint where they can quickly decide if they want to investigate it further or just move on.

Second, hashtags can be used to make your content more personable. Hashtags are highly effective in conveying your mood or emotions about a particular topic or event at any given moment, giving people a glimpse of your personality. You are not all business all the time and hashtags help express the whole person that you really are. Like code, hashtags express how you are feeling as you experience life. Hashtags are a helpful add-on to content you create or curate to help attract people with similar interests.

Misuse of hashtags can be a personal brand faux pas that could unintentionally do harm to your brand, which is most certainly not what you had in mind. Here are three tips for making hashtags work for you, as opposed to against you.

- *Check hashtags before using*—You can see whether a hashtag you plan to use is active by searching it on the platform where you plan to use it (e.g., Twitter or Instagram). The more posts that include a particular hashtag, the greater the potential reach of your messages. If there is not much activity associated with a particular hashtag, though, that does not necessarily mean you should not use it. Just understand that it may have less impact than a more popular hashtag option.

- *Use relevant hashtags*—Tagging content with frequently-used hashtags is less important than making sure your hashtags are relevant to the subject matter. Do not try to trick people into viewing your content by using hashtags only because they are popular. In general, the goal should be to find the right audience of people with shared interests. Also, industry-specific keywords or terms are good potential hashtags. For example, if your field is advertising, and you blog and share articles about trends and news in your field, an appropriate hashtag might be simply #advertising.

- *Use hashtags with care*—Keep in mind the main reason for using hashtags, which is to signal to others the topic of your content and to succinctly advertise that it might be interesting to them. Some hashtag users try to be overly clever, sprinkling hashtags throughout a post. Bear in mind that many people are turned off by too many hashtags. A good general rule to apply is to use only one or two hashtags to tag any given piece of content.

Engagement. In contrast to video and hashtags, which focus on pushing your content out to a desired audience, engagement is a concept more concerned with being a consumer of content created or curated by others.

Remember the mantra "give to get?" It applies to maximizing the impact of social media in your content marketing efforts, too. One way to raise the profile of your brand is to be an active participant on the social web. Sharing others' content that you find useful and giving feedback to others are just two examples of engagement that show your brand is not just concerned with one-way broadcasting of your information. It also shows that you are in tune with topics and conversations that matter to people with interests similar to yours. Sharing and commenting on others' content is also beneficial because other people who may not be connected with you in social media channels may finally become aware of you as a result of your shares or comments.

So, how should your engagement activity compare with creating and posting your own content? Opinions abound on how to allocate your time in engaging versus creating. One ratio for managing your social media and content creation/curation efforts is the 5-3-2 rule. This rule suggests that for every ten social media interactions you have, five should involve sharing content of others, three should be content related to your professional brand, and two should be personal posts. This mix places a premium on engaging with your network and beyond. It also lessens the risk that you inadvertently focus on self-promotion.[12]

The 5-3-2 rule is simple to understand but can be challenging to implement. You must commit to the "give to get" mindset by scheduling time daily to read content on social media sites and blogs so that you can give feedback, ask questions, and share the work of others that might be beneficial to people in your network.

Feeding Your Content Machine

You may have bought into the benefits of a content creation strategy to market your personal brand but still remain uncertain about one important detail: How to create the content. What will you write about? What sources of information will you draw upon to learn? Writing blog posts, producing videos or podcasts, and posting to social media is not as simple as flipping a switch and having ideas flow. You have to fuel your content machine.

Marketing expert Danny Sullivan, co-founder of the websites Search Engine Land and Marketing Land, estimates that he reads up to four hours each day to conduct research that influences his writing.[13] That amount of time might seem unrealistic if you have a full schedule already (and you probably do!). The point here is less about the exact amount of time devoted to reading and learning every day and more about having a commitment to reading and learning to some degree on a daily basis.

Three tools to filter information online to quickly and efficiently find relevant content are Google Alerts, news readers, and hashtags.

Google Alerts

If you are like the majority of Internet users, you know all about Google's capabilities to deliver a vast number of results related to search queries from web pages to images, video, news, and more. Generally speaking, Google delivers (instantly) more information than you could possibly ever sift through daily to find content you want to and need to devour. You need to winnow your results to more specific outcomes.

Luckily, you can harness the power of Google to deliver links exclusively on specific topics of interest by using Google Alerts. This service allows you to receive emails with links to content related solely to alerts you create. Alerts can be set to receive updates on content from different sources (blogs, news, web pages, video, books, or discussions), different frequencies (as content is posted, daily, or weekly), languages, regions, and even quality (best results or all results).

Staying abreast of current news and conversations about your industry is made easier by Google Alerts. Content comes to you rather than you searching the vastness of Google to find it online.

Google Alerts can also be used to find company-specific content. Similar to the way you can set up alerts for particular topics, you can also set up alerts to receive updates about specific companies. For example, setting an alert for "Coca-Cola" would return updates on content related on a daily basis only to that company. Use of Google Alerts to monitor content about companies can be taken one step further by setting up alerts for job opportunities with a particular company. So, in the Coca-Cola example, setting an alert for "*jobs Coca-Cola*" would begin to return links daily to any content posted about jobs with Coca-Cola.

One more way to use Google Alerts to identify relevant content is to set Google Alerts for specific people in your field who are written about or quoted frequently in news stories, or who publish their own content. For example, if you want to build expertise in consumer electronics products, or specifically about a company such as Apple, you might set up an alert to receive updates about Apple's CEO, Tim Cook. You'll never miss a relevant piece of news ever again!

News Readers

The Google Alerts tool is not the only way to collect topic-specific information that will help you stay current on news and developments related to your passions and professional objectives. Many different types of news readers are also available that curate, or collect content related to your interests and make that content readily available at your fingertips. Four news readers that deliver content but which vary in the format it is packaged are Feedly, Paper.Li, Flipboard, and LinkedIn Pulse.

Feedly. Feedly is a popular tool for distributing content from websites that update frequently (such as blogs). New content is delivered through rich site summary (RSS), perhaps better known as real simple syndication. Feedly lets you enter website URLs from which you wish to receive updated content as published. The benefit of RSS feeds is that new content from your favorite websites comes to you rather than you having to visit websites frequently to see if any new content has been posted. Feedly is available for desktop computers, tablets, and smartphones.

Paper.Li. You can benefit from the social sharing of others using the service Paper.Li. It is positioned as an online newspaper, with users creating publications based on their interests (general topics like politics and sports) as well as professional interests (like civil engineering and healthcare management.) You can read newspapers on the Paper.Li website, or subscribe to papers and have links to new editions delivered to you via email. Paper.Li is a content sharing tool, meaning you can use it to consume information or become a publisher yourself and share content.

Flipboard. If you like reading content in a magazine-style format, Flipboard is a tool you will likely enjoy using. Like Paper.Li, Flipboard is based on content sharing. Use it to follow magazines created by other users, or to create magazines to share content with others. For example, I (Don) publish magazines to share current events in marketing with my students, as well as publish a magazine on personal branding (Personal Branding U) to share articles about managing the world's most important brands. Flipboard is available on iOS, Android, and Windows mobile devices, as well as desktop computers.

LinkedIn Pulse. LinkedIn Pulse was explored in depth in an earlier chapter as a helpful platform for publishing content in blog form to share one's expertise and reach a wider audience. Also discussed was using Pulse as part of a learning plan for strengthening brand Makeup. Pulse is like a news reader in that it curates posts across the LinkedIn network sorted by topic (e.g., education, careers, and technology). Consumers can then select to follow high-profile individuals, who are referred to as influencers, and who are known for being experts in their respective fields. Examples would include media publishers like *The New York Times* or Yahoo! News, or any LinkedIn member publishing on Pulse. If you are using LinkedIn for managing other aspects of your personal brand such as networking and communicating your brand value (and you should be!), you must also take advantage of the content available on Pulse to build a foundation for content creation as well.

Hashtags

Social media activity can be filtered to help you find useful content that you might otherwise miss. The use of hashtags as a filtering tool was touched on briefly earlier in this chapter but deserves mention again.

The use of hashtags brings valuable organization to what can be a cluttered mass of posts on your Twitter or other social networking site feeds. Following hashtags related to your interests can be simplified by using a service that displays posts by hashtags. Hootsuite and TweetDeck are two such services.

Hootsuite users can follow different hashtags, as well as Twitter lists presented in real-time called streams. Hootsuite can be used as a dashboard to follow feeds and updates on Twitter, Facebook, Google+, and

WordPress. Similarly, TweetDeck, a service owned by Twitter, is a dashboard that lets you monitor streams of Twitter hashtag activity in real time. Hashtags serve as shortcuts to content that is of interest to you rather than wading through all posts in your feed; that said, a little technological help navigating the sea of hashtags using these services can be quite beneficial!

Making the Most of Content Marketing

We established early on that marketing your personal brand is not a project with a beginning and end, but rather is an ongoing endeavor requiring commitment to maintain and build. Content marketing is no exception—once you flip the switch and turn on your content machine, it must be regularly utilized in support of your personal brand.

Rather than being overwhelmed by the thought of always having to be consuming, creating, and curating content, embrace the possibilities that content marketing offers for your personal brand building efforts. Apply the following three principles to make producing your content your joy and your ally, not a pain, in achieving your brand building goals:

- *Have a strategy*—The channels and tools available for producing and gathering content shared in this chapter will do little to advance your brand unless you have goals in place for using them. Ask the question "What do I want to accomplish through content marketing?" Sharing expertise, helping other people, and expanding the size of your professional network are three examples of outcomes that can be connected to your effective use of content marketing. Knowing what you want and expect to happen before you begin is vitally important so that you do not invest a great deal of time in content channels then fail to achieve clear results that reward your efforts.

- *Schedule time*—Build time into your daily schedule for content marketing. Be selective about the number of social media channels you use given that there are so many of them and you are probably limited in the amount of time you can allocate to participation. The same applies for content creation, sharing, and reading. Carve out a part of your day for content marketing, realizing that it is valuable activity for developing your brand Message and Makeup.

- *Give to get*—This mantra has been repeated several times in this chapter, but it is worth mentioning once again. The value in content marketing is the benefit others receive from you. Your purpose for sharing ideas or information is to help others. Building your own brand is a by-product of your willingness to be a resource to others. Practice the 5-3-2 Rule or some other method that emphasizes engaging and helping people.

Take Action

Take these important actions and ask yourself these important questions before we proceed with the process of building your personal brand.

1. Develop a plan to implement the 5-3-2 rule (5 shares, 3 original posts, 2 personal posts) for using content marketing with your personal brand. For shares, decide which sources (e.g., magazines, trade journals, blogs, websites, or social networking sites) you will rely on to gather information to share with others.

   For original content, ask yourself what topics and content channel(s) will be the focus of your original content. For personal content, what aspect or aspects of your personal life outside of your profession do you believe others would find interesting or relate to in some way?

2. Create a weekly reading/learning plan that will expand your sources of shareable content and inspire creation of original content.

   First, schedule one hour a day for reading/learning. It can be a one-hour block or segments of twenty or thirty minutes. If it is hard to come up with one hour, think about your typical day. Are you spending time on non-essential tasks that can be devoted to reading/learning instead?

Second, decide which tools for gathering topic-specific content you will use (Google Alerts, news readers, hashtags). If you have not used these tools before, try them out (they are all free) to determine which ones you find easiest to use or the most valuable for delivering useful content

16.

CAPTURING YOUR PERSONAL BRAND IN A RÉSUMÉ

"Be a person, not a résumé."
—Sharad Vivek Sagar

This quote from Sagar, a social entrepreneur whose passion is to create educational opportunities for kids, may at first seem inconsistent with the theme of this chapter. But it's not.

Sagar's point is you should not become so consumed with the process and content of résumé creation that it overshadows the bigger purpose, which is to articulate your brand value in a succinct and persuasive manner.

A résumé is one communication tool in your brand Message toolkit—nothing more and nothing less. It is most certainly not a magic ticket to opportunity, but rather, an overview of what you have to offer by way of revealing glimpses of your brand Meaning and a summary of credentials, skills, and experiences that comprise your brand Makeup. Because if brand Meaning and Makeup are not given priority, the story of "Brand You," as told by your résumé, could be one that potential employers or clients find uninteresting or incompatible with their needs.

Working on writing a résumé without first giving attention to the details of building out brand Meaning and Makeup would be like creating an advertisement for a product that has yet to be invented. The message would be incomplete and unclear because the product's attributes and performance capabilities are as of yet also unknown.

Keeping in mind this disclaimer about what a résumé can and cannot accomplish, let's now ponder how a résumé and other personal brand communication tactics can be effective brand Message tools.

Evolution of the Résumé

The custom of using a résumé to showcase one's background and credentials is actually a relatively new phenomenon in the workplace.

219

The first résumé can be traced back to the late 1400s and was written by (of all people) artist Leonardo da Vinci. It is believed the original purpose of the modern résumé was to serve as a letter of introduction to one's acquaintances.

Use of résumés in the modern business world can be traced back to the 1930s. At that time of their inception, their style was quite informal, often written on scraps of paper. In some ways, they resembled today's Facebook profile, containing personal information like marital status, religion, and even height and weight.

By the 1950s, a résumé became an expected contribution from job applicants. The availability of typewriters in the 1970s enabled people to create more professional looking résumés. Later, adoption of word processing programs on personal computers gave résumé writers more creative options for formatting and presentation. Then in 1994, the World Wide Web gave recruiters and job candidates global access to their audiences. Monster and CareerBuilder later emerged as early leaders in the online job website category. Email became another distribution channel for sending and receiving résumés shortly thereafter. Résumés finally went social with the founding of LinkedIn in 2003. YouTube gave job seekers another medium to deliver résumé information when it launched in 2007.[1]

The practice of sending a hard copy of a résumé and cover letter has been largely replaced by either emailing a résumé or uploading it to a website with applicant tracking software (ATS) that helps employers manage the inflow of job applications. As such, it is easier than ever to distribute your résumé, but in turn it is harder and harder to stand out among a pack other applicants.

This dilemma means it is crucial that you carefully craft your résumé so that it is less likely to get filtered out or otherwise ignored.

Anatomy of an Effective Résumé

Opinions vary greatly regarding how exactly to write a résumé. Most people would agree, though, that the following four considerations must be addressed effectively in order to give your résumé any chance to rise above the rest: Formatting, positioning, content, and copywriting.

Formatting

Before we get to the actual content of your résumé, let's cover some frequently asked questions related to proper formatting of the document. These questions deal with length, margins, font, and alignment of résumé content.

Length. Perhaps the most debated element of a résumé is length. The general consensus is that your résumé should be no longer than one page. Begin the writing process by understanding that your goal is to tell the story of "Brand You" in a single page (we will get into what content to include or exclude shortly). An exception to the one-page limit is if you are many years into a professional career or if you need to create a more detailed chronology of activities and accomplishments. The format this type of document takes on is known as a curriculum vitae, or CV. But in most situations, the document of choice is the simpler, more straightforward résumé.

Margins. The decision on margin settings is important as you strive to keep your résumé to a maximum of one page. Many résumé writing resources recommend margins of between one-half inch and one inch on all sides. A benefit of using a wide margin is the effect that white space has or creates on the overall appearance and readability of the document. A résumé utilizing generous white space like one-inch margins is a more visually pleasing presentation because it is far less cluttered than a document with (for instance) one-half inch margins. Job applicants understandably want to jam as many of their accomplishments as possible on a single page. But the content on the page has a better chance of being actually read and understood if it is presented in a clear, less dizzying format. White space is your friend!

Font. Two considerations for the ideal font to use are size and type. Font size is recommended in the range of 10-12 point, with the same font size used consistently throughout the résumé. The lone exception is that your name at the top of the page should be presented in a larger font size than the rest of your text. Use bold font to enhance structure and presentation, such as for section headings or to highlight specific skills or achievements. Be careful not to overuse bold font, though. Use it sparingly enough to make it work for you, either to enhance organization or to emphasize key points. As far as which font to use, easy-to-read fonts such as Arial, Tahoma, Times New Roman, or Verdana are recommended. Avoid the temptation to use overly fancy or stylistic fonts. Remember that the goal for formatting your résumé is to make it as easy as possible for someone to read and process the information!

Alignment. Manage the visual aesthetic of your résumé by ensuring that alignment of your headings and the text beneath each heading follows a consistent alignment pattern or scheme. For example, if you have subheadings under a main heading "Experience" for "Work Experience," "Internships," and/or "Volunteerism," make sure all three headings have the same indentation and spacing between subsections. Another alignment issue is how information is presented in headings. It is recommended that the presentation of information about each job or position held be in the order of employer name, job title, and dates. The reason is that applicant tracking system software typically looks for company name first. If you begin with dates instead, it may misread the information you are trying to convey.[2]

Positioning Statement

For many years, the standard opening for a résumé was a statement of objective. The purpose of this leadoff statement was to clearly express what one wanted to achieve or to become professionally, either in the short-term or on a longer-time continuum.

Objective statements, however, have fallen out of favor among recruiters and résumé writing experts for two reasons. First, the sameness of many objective statements rendered them meaningless. Too many people were making similar, vague proclamations and communicating very little about their potential value to a prospective employer. Over time, as a result of this, the objective statement became essentially wasted space and effort. Second, an objective statement is now considered ineffective because its focus is wrongheaded—highlighting what the applicant wants, not how the applicant could potentially benefit the employer.

Here are two examples that make the case for why objective statements simply must go (or have gone) the way of the dinosaur:

- "To secure a position with a well-established organization with a stable environment that will lead to a lasting relationship in the field of finance."

- "To obtain a position that will enable me to use my strong organizational skills, educational background, and ability to work well with people."[3]

Objective statements like these are flat-out useless since it is already understood that getting a job is the objective! The real content that should be offered in this prime résumé real estate (and we will discuss soon in what form to shape it) is what a you possess in abilities and upside that sets you apart from other prospective candidates in terms of the value you can create once hired for the job.

The objective statement may be out of fashion, but an attention grabbing lead is still needed. Not surprisingly, the answer to how to craft the perfect lead-in statement to your résumé can be found in your brand Makeup, meaning how you have positioned your brand.

Remember that in Chapter 11, you learned the importance of creating a distinctive brand position, different approaches for positioning your brand, and hopefully, writing your own brand positioning statement. One benefit of defining brand position is that it becomes part of your brand Message. It is how you articulate your Meaning and Makeup.

In contrast to the bland objective statements proffered in the previous paragraphs, notice how a positioning statement fueled by one's innate sense of personal brand positioning vigorously communicates what a person can do rather than what he or she wants to do:

- "Award-winning website designer, adept in the latest programming languages, managing project teams, and growing clientele."

- "Passionate about growing as a professional and using my talents in the community."

Of course, whatever brand positioning statement you write must meet the criteria of containing real and relevant differentiation points, as discussed in Chapter 11. Always keep in mind that the goal of a positioning statement is to convey a summary of the attributes of "Brand You" and the benefits you can deliver. Whether you label it "Positioning Statement" or "Summary," you need a concise description of your value as a lead-in to more detailed information on your résumé.

Organization and Structure

One of the most challenging aspects of writing a résumé is the conflicting advice offered about what to include and what to exclude from your one-page brand story.

As was previously mentioned, you will find many different opinions about résumé content. As we conducted research for this book (and we were quite aware beforehand of the widely divergent views on résumés), even we were surprised at the degree of debate that exist about "right" and "wrong" résumé content among top sources and experts.

With that said, however, the following offers our best thinking on what to include on your résumé. Specifically, we address common content sections: experience, education, skills, honors, and professional memberships.

Experience. The lead-off section for the typical résumé details prior work experience. The exception to leading with work experience is if you are a student or recent college graduate. In those cases, you probably lack extensive professional experiences to tout and are better off marketing yourself for the current and cutting-edge education and training you now possess in your brand Makeup. If you are a more seasoned professional, though, limit the overview of work experience to the past 10-15 years. (That time frame might be more like five years if you are a more recent college graduate.)

The content of the Experience section should include:

- Dates of employment, using only starting and ending years (e.g., 2012-2016). It is unnecessary to include the specific month with the year. Omitting months may also help mask small gaps in your employment history that (regardless of circumstances) could be troubling to a prospective employer (or a convenient excuse to pass over you in an especially crowded, highly competitive candidate pool).

- List experience for each position held using bullet points rather than a paragraph approach. Doing so will make for an easier read for the person (or software!) evaluating your résumé. Bullet points should focus on outputs (results and outcomes) more so than inputs (assigned duties and tasks). More guidance on how to present experience will be shared in the next section on copywriting.

- Honors or awards received related to job performance.

- If you did an internship, position it as work experience rather than education (even if you did it for course credit). Again, focus on outputs (skills developed or results achieved) just as you would when summarizing a permanent position held.

- If you have performed volunteer work related to your field (e.g., a web designer building a web page for a local nonprofit organization), or picked up new skills through volunteering, position these as relevant experience. If you have significant volunteer service that is unrelated to your profession or field, consider creating a separate section titled Volunteerism on your résumé. If you helped with an adult literacy program over the past five years, for example, that is certainly a part of your brand story that needs to be told; but it is better suited for a separate section of the résumé.

Education. This section should follow Experience except, as previously mentioned, in the case of a student or new graduate. Information in this section should include:

- Degree or degrees earned, major, institution, and dates of study. Be sure to use the full name of the degree and not just the initials (Bachelor of Arts instead of B.A.).

- Grade Point Average should be included only if it makes you more marketable. A general rule is to include overall GPA only if it is a 3.0 or higher.

- List notable educational projects or activities but not courses taken. Avoid listing specific courses taken because thousands of other students took those same classes. Only make an exception to this rule if it is to share information about a particular course experience that helped shape or develop specific hard or soft skills. An employer will have much more interest in specific projects you may have completed within the courses you took. For example, if you took an advertising campaigns course and worked on a team that created a campaign for a business or nonprofit organization, include that information and highlight the role you played in the project.

- List extracurricular activities such as fraternity/sorority involvement, student organization participation, or student government connections. Again, focus on outputs (e.g., leadership positions held, project participation, or other accomplishments) rather than simply inputs. Listing membership in organizations does not communicate involvement or the growth you experienced (or that the organization experienced resulting from your engagement in it!)

Skills. Your experience and education give hiring managers a glimpse into your preparation for a position. Summarizing the hard and soft skills you possess presents a much more complete picture of your brand Makeup and how you could potentially contribute to the organization seeking help. Revisit the discussion of hard skills and soft skills in Chapter 8, as well as the personal inventory you took to determine preparedness for your field.

Be sure to include any certifications earned, as they are tangible evidence of hard skills. For example, a graphic design student who earns certification in Visual Communication using Adobe Photoshop has proof of competency using Adobe Photoshop that someone who merely lists Adobe Photoshop as a skill cannot demonstrate. A word of caution that must be given, though, is that you must only list skills and certifications that you have actually acquired or can demonstrate. In other words, don't lie or even fudge the truth! The truth will come out eventually!

Exclusions. Thus far, we have focused on what to include in the content of your résumé. Here's what you should leave out:

- *Address.* In some instances, including your address on a résumé could lead to a company excluding you from consideration (even though human relations policy may not allow that). Why? For instance, if you do not live in the same area where the job is located, an employer might question your degree of willingness to relocate in order to take the job. A long commute to work could also create concern that drive time could take away from a candidate's work time. Outside of these situations, including your address is acceptable. However, that space might be better utilized by providing an active link to your LinkedIn profile, personal website, or other destination that would give a company greater insight into the true you.

- *General skills.* You are not going to impress an employer if you list Microsoft Office as one of your hard skills. It, and others like it, are competencies that are a given for many positions.

- *Personal information.* Employers are prohibited from asking you about age, marital status, or religion. Divulging this information could hurt how you are perceived if a hiring manager has negative biases toward any of these demographic characteristics.

- *"References available upon request."* Many résumés end with this unnecessary statement. It is understood that if a company wants to contact references, you will supply them with a list of people who can speak about your Meaning and Makeup. Don't waste valuable space on your résumé with this statement.

The content of the Experience, Education, and Skills sections is like a marketing brochure for "Brand You." Make sure that the most compelling parts of your brand story are included!

Copywriting

The reality of résumé writing today is that you are writing to satisfy two audiences. One is human and one is software.

Of course, you want your résumé to catch the attention of a hiring manager, supervisor, or business owner whose perceptions of you are crucial in determining if you are a potential fit for their organization. Increasingly, though, it is important to write your résumé in a tone and style that meets the criteria for a position set by applicant tracking software (ATS).

One estimate puts ATS utilization at seventy-five percent of large companies.[4] An ATS identifies prospective employees by matching keywords in a job posting to the appearance of those keywords in an applicant's résumé. Applicants are ranked based on how closely a candidate's résumé matches each keyword and how many of the keyword phrases a résumé contains.

Whether you upload your résumé to an ATS to be screened or you deliver it in person, some writing fundamentals will be the same. In résumé writing, you are trying to communicate how you would make for a solid match or fit to the organization's present and future needs. Thus, you could benefit by taking on the mindset of a copywriter.

In marketing, the task of a copywriter is to create written communication that informs, entertains, or persuades through channels such as print ads, brochures, or web pages. Similarly, the objective of your résumé is to inform the recipient of your brand Makeup and to persuade him or her to realize the value you offer.

Two copywriting tactics that will serve you well are optimization and using words that sell value.

Optimization. Your résumé is not a one-size-fits-all sales brochure for your brand. The message must be tailored to each recipient, whether it is an organization or a person. This tactic is known as optimization, defined as customizing the content and language of your résumé to the specific recipient. The importance of optimization has already been established if your résumé is uploaded in an ATS. The same principle applies if your résumé is ready by humans as well. In either situation, the following tactics can optimize the content of your résumé:

- Use keywords that are consistent with the terminology and language of the industry you aspire to join.

- Write headlines that emphasize accomplishments rather than making company/title the focal point.

- Include relevant hyperlinks to articles you have written, your personal website, a video resume, or portfolio.

- Include links to social media profiles, beginning with LinkedIn, as well as other sites you use for professional purposes.

- Streamline content by using active voice, eliminating "fluff" and clichés, and using hard facts or statistical data to communicate value.[5]

If you feel that optimization is an attempt to "game" the system, you are right (sort of). The system (specifically an ATS) is designed to identify résumés whose content matches what the other party wants. That is not gaming the system. That is meeting the needs of the buyer (or more specifically, the employer).

Words that Communicate Value. A second tactic for enhancing your résumé as a persuasive communication piece is to focus on using words that convey job-appropriate capabilities and accomplishments.

As a summary of your education and experience, it is common for a résumé to become a listing of schools attended, degrees earned, prior employment, job titles, and tasks performed. Although this information may be an accurate portrayal of what you have done in the past, it does little to convince a recruiter or manager of the value you could bring to their organization in the future (hopefully the near future!).

Avoid the trap of allowing your résumé to become a predictable summary listing of your past accomplishments by placing emphasis on results that occurred as a result of your work instead. Yes, you will need to list employer organization name and job titles held for each experience-related entry on your résumé; but your description of the experience becomes part of your brand story.

Said another way, forego listing tasks performed and instead summarize results achieved. For example, a résumé of a candidate for a sales position that contains bullet points such as "named Salesperson of the Month four times" and "retained an average of 97% of clients each year" provides compelling evidence of a prospect's capabilities (meaning what they could do on a future job as well). Stating results does more to

229

communicate your value than a simple laundry list of job duties performed (a list that every other person in a similar job could probably create as well).

See Figure 16.1 for examples of action words to use in your résumé that will better emphasize your capabilities. Remember that the aim is to communicate what you have done or achieved, so choose words that properly sell your value!

Advanced	Implemented	Recommended
Attained	Increased	Retained
Budgeted	Initiated	Saved
Closed	Mentored	Secured
Designed	Multiplied	Supported
Developed	Negotiated	Streamlined
Exceeded	Operated	Taught
Generated	Obtained	Trained
Guided	Presented	Updated
Hosted	Provided	Validated

Source: "Top 100 Most Powerful Resume Words" (2013), April 8, retrieved from http://www.careerealism.com/top-resume-words/.

Figure 16.1 Action Words that Communicate Value

Complementary Pieces to Your Résumé

You may have written your first résumé as early as during your high school years and have continued to update it for the duration of your professional career. There's no question that even today, the traditional résumé remains the single most important personal branding document you will create.

As important as a résumé is to your personal branding efforts, though, it is not the only marketing tool at your disposal. Other means of communicating your value can and should also be strategically leveraged.

Three tools that can be incorporated into brand Message to complement your résumé are a cover letter, video résumé, and infographic résumé. Many books have been written about each of these tools, so the

230

aim here is to simply give an overview of their value so you can decide for yourself whether or not you want to learn more about each option.

Cover Letter

A cover letter is a companion piece to the traditional résumé. Although many organizations use online application processes to gather résumés, it is often possible to upload additional files such as a cover letter as well.

Think of writing a cover letter as a given; you want to write one to go along with your résumé anytime you apply for a job. Regardless of whether you are applying through an online system or a connection in your professional network, a human being will be reviewing your résumé sooner or later. Do not miss the opportunity to go beyond the one-page summary that your résumé provides and always write a cover letter that adds to your sales pitch.

One way to think of a cover letter is that it is a door opener, telling hiring managers more about who you are and why they should consider you for the job opening. An effective cover letter conveys three ideas:

- Why you want to work for the organization.
- Specific ways your expertise can benefit the organization.
- What makes you different from competing candidates?[6]

Although these sources of added value can be inferred from a résumé, take advantage of the opportunity to tell your story more directly using a cover letter that lets you further tailor the presentation of your case to a prospective employer.

As with other brand Message documents, many opinions exist about what information a cover letter should and should not contain. You will likely encounter other opinions if you do your own research on this topic, but here is our collective take on proper and necessary cover letter content.

Cover Letter Dos. Be sure your cover letter meets the following criteria:

- Maximum length should be one page, with the letter consisting of three paragraphs.

- Address the letter to a specific person. Do research or make a phone call to the organization to find out who the appropriate person is to whom you should address the letter. This tactic is consistent with the idea of tailoring a cover letter to the organization.

- State in first paragraph why you want to work for the organization.

- Use the second paragraph to provide specific examples of your abilities and how you could use them specifically to add value to the organization to which you are applying.

- Include a call to action in the third and concluding paragraph. State your intention to follow up on your application (e.g., "I will phone you next week...").

- Ensure that the content of your cover letter is grammatically correct and error free.[7]

Cover Letter Don'ts. Avoid the following missteps that could result in your cover letter negatively impacting your chances of being considered for a position:

- *Don't overuse the word "I."* Focus on benefits of "Brand You" to the organization, meaning what's in it for them if you are selected.

- *Don't begin with a weak opening.* Avoid overused and uninspiring openers like "I am writing..." or "Please consider me..." They know you are writing and of course you want to be considered...or else you would not write! Lead your cover letter off instead with a sincere statement about why you want to work for the organization (e.g., *"Zappos has a reputation for stellar customer service. Your company's concern for employees and customers resonates with my desire to serve others and bring happiness to those with whom I interact"*).

- *Don't omit top selling points about you that are a perfect match for the position.* Your résumé only summarizes your qualifications. It cannot tell your story as a tailored description of how your expertise could benefit the organization.

- *Don't repeat your résumé word for word.* A lazy approach to writing a cover letter is simply restating in statement form what is already bulleted information contained in the résumé. Think of the cover letter as a blank canvas to gain the attention of a hiring manager with information such as a reference to a mutual connection in your professional networks, explaining your intention to change careers or move to a new geographic area, and/or organization-specific information that shows you did your homework about how perfect a fit you will make in the organization.

- *Don't end on a passive note.* Remember that you are selling yourself. A salesperson would never make a presentation without suggesting that the prospective buyer take action. As stated earlier, conclude your cover letter with a call to action to let the recipient know that you intend to follow up. Otherwise, you are left to hope that you will get a follow-up call or email. Assert yourself by stating your intent to take follow-up action.[8]

Keep in mind that you will encounter different opinions about what to include or leave out of a cover letter. You will even encounter the opinion that cover letters are irrelevant today! Our recommendation is that you take advantage of the communication tools available to sell your value... including the use of a cover letter.

Video Résumé

More information is being delivered via video as technology improvements have enabled faster-loading, higher-quality viewing experiences on smartphones, tablets, and computers.

The rise of online video consumption could be an opportunity for you to show off your personality while also expressing the benefits you can offer up to a potential employer. A survey of employers concerning video résumés found that 89% were receptive to viewing video résumés.

Before you grab a video camera, though, it must be noted that receptiveness does not equal behavior; only 17% said they had actually viewed an applicant's video résumé.[9] Despite the relatively low percentage of hiring managers who said they had viewed a video résumé, the fact that video viewing is becoming more commonplace should have you considering how you could use this tool to your advantage.

A well-planned and produced video résumé could help you stand out among an applicant pool that has limited its self-marketing efforts to producing a traditional print résumé. On the other hand, a poorly executed video résumé could be a turn-off to your personal brand and eliminate you from consideration for jobs. Apply the following advice to make your video résumé work for you:

- *Be prepared.* Know what you will say and practice it prior to shooting the video.

- *Dress professionally.* Even though you may be shooting video in your bedroom, dress as if you are in the boardroom.

- *Keep it short.* The suggested time frame is one to two minutes, maximum. If you watch videos online, think about what you are inclined to do if a video is more than a few minutes long. You do not watch it (or at least not all of it) unless it is really entertaining and relevant! Your message should be brief to reduce the risk of losing viewer interest.

- *Begin by introducing yourself.* State your first name and last name, just as you would if you were meeting someone face-to-face.

- *Summarize why you would be a good employee.* Touch on the skills you possess, past accomplishments, and the value you could bring to the organization.

- *Keep it all business.* Do not mix personal content with the marketing of your professional brand.
- *Close with call to action.* Thank the viewer for taking the time to watch your video and include a call to action (e.g., show a URL to your personal website or LinkedIn profile).[10]

Once you have created a video résumé, you might be wondering what you should do with it in terms of distribution. One benefit of having a personal website (as discussed earlier in this chapter) is that you own the real estate and can post whatever you want. A video résumé is ideal content to post to your website. Also, posting video to your LinkedIn profile (also covered earlier in this chapter) is a clear way to stand out from the pack. Finally, some job websites allow users to post video. If that is an option, take advantage of it.

Infographic Résumé

Another visual format for communicating information found in a traditional résumé is an infographic.

You likely have seen infographics on websites, in blog posts, or on social media sites. An infographic is a chart or diagram used to communicate information visually (as opposed to in a traditionally written or paragraph form). An infographic resume can be appealing given that we are accustomed to highly visual environments in this day and age. It may not be ideal for every industry or position, nor is it a replacement for a text résumé, but it might just be the add-on to your job search that gives you the final competitive edge.

An infographic can be especially effective for communicating numerical or statistical info. For positions that require creativity or design skills, an infographic résumé can obviously be a huge plus, as it can essentially serve as a sample of the creative abilities you could bring to the job. It is advised that an infographic résumé be submitted along with a traditional résumé, as hiring managers will prefer to also look at a standard format document to adequately size up your experience and education.

Charts can be embedded in an infographic to communicate depth or level of skill possessed, but they may be confusing to a reader since many skills are hard to describe numerically. Thus, charts should be kept simple so that they are more likely to be understood.

The color scheme used is important as certain colors evoke feelings (e.g., blue and green elicit trust). Be deliberate in the color scheme used. For example, you could use the brand colors of a company if you prepare an infographic specifically to apply for a position with that company. Do not select colors randomly; color choices should aid in making your infographic easy to read and visually appealing. A light background with multiple tones of a single color is a preferred approach when using color.[11]

If you decide to produce an infographic to complement your résumé, keep in mind that an infographic can make you stand out... for better or worse. A creative, clean infographic design can make you stand out positively among a crowd of applicants for a position. A poorly conceived infographic, though, could make you stand out as someone the recipient definitely would not want to hire.

Given, the importance of getting infographic design right, here are seven elements to consider including in your infographic résumé:

- *Headline/tagline.* Infographics have a theme and title. Your infographic résumé is no different. Think like a copywriter (as encouraged earlier in this chapter) to write a headline that communicates your value or the benefits of hiring you.

- *Photo.* A professional-looking photo personalizes your infographic, showing the recipient the "real you" that is not communicated on a traditional résumé.

- *Timeline.* If you want to present education and work experience events in chronological order, you can use a timeline to show education and employment history, as well as accomplishments like dates of receiving scholarships or winning awards.

- *Quotes or references.* Let the words of those who know you best sell your value in the form of testimonials from customers, bosses, colleagues, or professors.

- *Statistics/Charts.* Accomplishments that can be quantified can be presented using statistics or in chart form for easy consumption.

- *Word clouds.* Another visual aid for showing relative magnitude is a word cloud. For traits that are more difficult to quantify, such as personal strengths and skills, a word cloud could visually show your dominant traits. A free online tool such as Wordle can be used to create a word cloud that visually emphasizes personal brand strengths.

- *Call to Action.* An effective close to an infographic résumé is to visually present online links that could be used to check out your presence on LinkedIn, your personal website, or social networking sites.

Creating an infographic résumé is not for everyone, and the thought of designing such a visual may be intimidating. But designing an infographic to tout your credentials could also be a difference maker if your chosen field is one in which hiring managers would be receptive to receiving information delivered visually.

Take Action

Ask yourself these important questions or take these actions before we proceed with the process of building your personal brand:

1. Assuming you have a résumé already, conduct a self-critique of it for formatting, positioning, content, and copywriting as described in this chapter. For each dimension, rate your résumé using a scale of 1-10, with anchors of "poor" and "excellent."

2. Also, ask someone else (e.g., a mentor, teacher, or trusted advisor) to use the same scale to evaluate the formatting, positioning, content, and copywriting of your résumé. Based on your self-rating and the feedback received from others, identify what improvements are needed to strengthen your résumé.

3. Write a cover letter aimed at a company you wish would hire you. Use the three-paragraph structure recommended in this chapter (a statement of why you want to work for the organization, examples of how your Makeup would benefit the organization, and a call to action). Be mindful of the cover letter "do's and don'ts" covered in this chapter. Ask the same person who critiqued your résumé (mentor, teacher, or advisor) for feedback on the cover letter as well.

PART FIVE: PUTTING IT ALL TOGETHER

17.

THE SECRET M: "MEASURE"

"If you can't measure it, you can't manage it."
—Peter F. Drucker

This book uses a framework called the "3 Ms" that is a specific, simple, yet powerful approach and if used properly will assist you in the development of your personal brand.

Remember, the first **M** was Meaning and it was about understanding the purpose, values and mission that guide what you do. Remember, the meaning must be first clear to you and be relevant to your life that you have lived on a daily basis.

Remember, the second **M** was Makeup and it was about combining traits, attitude and training that are potential sources of value for the people that you serve. As you learned, Makeup played off meaning and is the extension of the purpose, values and mission seen in the knowledge and skills needed to compete in your chosen profession.

Remember, the third **M** was Message and it was about communicating your brand through face – to face interaction and online presences. And as you found out message is all about communication and translating words on paper to daily action!

If you complete the steps in this framework you may realize that each **M** makes up the title of this book – **Me**! Taking the proper steps of building meaning, makeup and message results in a better understanding of the most important person in the room – you. That why we named the book *Me: How to Sell Who You Are, What You Do, and Why You Matter to the World.*

Is it That Simple?

But it is it that simple? Can the framework alone help develop your personal brand so that it becomes a competitive advantage for you in the marketplace? We think so, but we have also added another dimension (measurement) to this book that if used correctly can speed up the adoption and retention of the information found within these pages and we call it the Secret M - Measurement.

The Secret M: Measure

Can you manage something that you don't measure? The answer is, "maybe." We believe that there is some truth to what Drucker said and further, that measurement allows for better, more informed decision making. While it can't guarantee the "right" or "best" decision, measuring, in almost every case, helps avoid a bad decision. The rest is up to what your "gut" says. In this case, measurement has taken the form as "personal assessment" which we believe its key to fully utilizing the content in this book.

Take Control

Marketing expert Seth Godin said "Many of us are taught to do our best and then let the world decide how to judge us. I think it's better to do your best and decide how you want to be judged and act that way."

By reading this book you have decided to take control of your personal branding process, and must work to build your reputation and your influence. Consider that one's reputation (your personal brand) is most frequently shaped by word of mouth. As you have learned, strategically positioning yourself as a contributor to others will not only enhance your reputation, but you will also be sought after by others.

If you are perceived as an expert (or would like to be), offer to share your wisdom with others by offering to train, coach, or even write about your expertise. Sometimes you have to take some risks and stretch, but make sure you properly prepare for the projects for which you volunteer. A job well done will lead to more opportunities to elevate yourself above the pack. That's what branding is all about!

Personal Assessment

The process of defining who you are begins with a personal assessment of your strengths and weaknesses. Consider your behavioral characteristics (mindset), the skills that you possess, and the expertise that you can demonstrate. Acknowledging how you communicate, how you behave as a team member, what type of leadership competence you exhibit, and what contributions you typically make during meetings or social activities are essential components of this process. All of these attributes and skills will influence how you are defined.

You are also defined based on the value you contribute to others. Can you articulate your personal value proposition and is it consistent with how those around you recognize your value contribution? A hard look in the mirror to confront these questions can be a difficult task, but it is one that is essential to the personal branding process.

Questions that you should be asking that are related to personal brand include:

- How are you different?
- How do you add value?
- Why should anyone listen to you?
- What are your life goals and do you have a plan?
- How are you reinventing yourself?
- How are you improving your skills?
- What steps are you taking to strategically position yourself as a prominent brand?
- How do others define who you are (parents, siblings, spouse, friends, colleagues, supervisors, and vendors)?
- Are you on "career cruise control" or are you committed to personal and professional growth?

Creating Your Plan

Your plan requires that you develop a vision and mission (remember Meaning). Determining who you want to be and shaping your destination are critical steps in the personal branding process. Setting clear goals and objectives and writing them down is simply a must. A list of action items will enable you to better and more quickly achieve your goals and objectives. If you want to be perceived as an expert, what steps must you take to develop your expertise? If you have the expertise, how can you position yourself as that expert?

In most cases, one must become a life-long learner. Gaining knowledge and developing skills is essential to becoming a true adder of value. Creating a personal growth plan and executing that plan is of utmost importance.

Staying the Course

As you continue the process of building your brand and your personal value proposition, keep in mind that the world around you and those people who populate it will continue to change. The interpersonal skills that are essential to building and enhancing relationships will be of the utmost importance as you continue to reinvent yourself and your brand in order to remain relevant. Paying close attention to the needs of those you serve will enable you to identify and then develop the necessary skills and expertise to best serve them over time. Strategically positioning the value that you can contribute to others and assisting them in achieving their goals will enhance your personal brand and provide an endless stream of exciting new opportunities.

We wish you much success in managing the world's most important brand.

NOTES

Chapter 1

1. "Fast Facts" (n.d.), retrieved from http://nces.ed.gov/fastfacts/display.asp?id=372.
2. Jordan Weissmann (2013), "How Bad is the Job Market for Job Grads? A Definitive Guide," April 4, retrieved from http://www.theatlantic.com/business/archive/2013/04/how-bad-is-the-job-market-for-college-grads-your-definitive-guide/274580/.
3. "Recent U.S. College Graduates Disillusioned, More than 40% Unemployed: Poll (2013), April 30, retrieved from http://www.theatlantic.com/business/archive/2013/04/how-bad-is-the-job-market-for-college-grads-your-definitive-guide/274580/.
4. B.L. Ochman (2013), "There Are 181,000 Social Media 'Gurus,' Ninjas,' 'Masters,' and 'Mavens' on Twitter," January 7, retrieved from http://adage.com/article/digitalnext/181-000-social-media-gurus-ninjas-masters-mavens-twitter/239026/.
5. Heather Huhman (2012), "Put Yourself in the Top 2 Percent of Job Seekers with a Personal Brand," September 16, retrieved from http://www.examiner.com/article/put-yourself-the-top-2-percent-of-job-seekers-with-a-personal-brand.

Chapter 2

1. "Quotes" (n.d.), retrieved from http://www.dizzydean.com/quotes.htm.
2. Jeff Bullas (2013), "21 Awesome Social Media Facts, Figures, and Statistics for 2013," May 5, retrieved from http://www.jeffbullas.com/2013/05/06/21-awesome-social-media-facts-figures-and-statistics-for-2013/.
3. "Dictionary" (2013), n.d., retrieved from http://www.marketingpower.com/_layouts/Dictionary.aspx.
4. Bob Minzesheimer (2011), "How the 'Oprah Effect' Changed Publishing," May 22, retrieved from http://usatoday30.usatoday.com/life/books/news/2011-05-22-Oprah-Winfrey-Book-Club_n.htm.

5. "Warren Buffet Joins Twitter, Gains 1,000 Followers a Minute" (2013), May 2, retrieved from http://news.yahoo.com/warren-buffett-joins-twitter-gains-10-000-followers-164619709.html.

6. Nicholas Scalice (2013), "5 Components of an Awesome Personal Brand," June 13, retrieved from https://medium.com/personal-branding/bf955590df24.

Chapter 3

1. "Dictionary" (2013), n.d., retrieved from http://www.marketingpower.com/_layouts/Dictionary.aspx.

2. Dale Carnegie (1936), *How to Win Friends and Influence People*, New York: Simon and Schuster.

3. "Search Engine Marketing Glossary of Terms," (2010), retrieved from http://www.sempo.org/learning_center/sem_glossary#b.

4. Stanley Hainsworth (2013), "What's Your Brand Promise?" April 5, retrieved from http://www.huffingtonpost.com/stanley-hainsworth/whats-your-brand-promise_b_3018105.html.

5. Hainsworth (2013).

6. Williams, Terrance (2010), "Are You Really 'Networking'?" February 4, retrieved from http://newgradlife.blogspot.com/2010/02/are-you-really-networking.html.

7. "That White Paper Guy's Bio" (2013), n.d., retrieved from http://www.thatwhitepaperguy.com/that-white-paper-guy-Gordon-Graham-bio.html.

8. Jennifer Aaker (1997), "Dimensions of Brand Personality," *Journal of Marketing Research*, 34 (3), 347-356.

9. "Our Heritage" (2013), n.d., retrieved from http://www.starbucks.com/about-us/our-heritage.

Chapter 4

1. "Self-Assessment: Career Values" (n.d.), retrieved from http://hrweb.berkeley.edu/learning/career-development/self-assessment/values.

2. Richard M. Ryan and Edward L. Deci (2000) "Intrinsic and Extrinsic Motivations: Classic Definitions and New Directions," *Contemporary Educational Psychology* 25, 54-67.

3. Kenneth Thomas (2009), "The Four Intrinsic Rewards that Drive Employee Engagement," *Ivey Business Journal*, December, retrieved from http://iveybusinessjournal.com/topics/the-workplace/the-four-intrinsic-rewards-that-drive-employee-engagement#.U149YFfZeil.

4. Ryan and Deci (2000)

5. Don Peppers (2014), "What Really Motivates You at Work?" February 3, retrieved from https://www.linkedin.com/today/post/article/20140203140253-17102372-what-really-motivates-you-at-work.

6. Thomas (2009)

7. Stephanie Krieg (2014), "Why Your Company Needs a Purpose Statement," May 7, retrieved from http://www.blogging4jobs.com/business/company-needs-purpose-statement/.

8. Todd Henry (n.d.), "7 Word Bio", retrieved from http://www.accidentalcreative.com/you/7-word-bio/.

Chapter 5

1. Richard Florida (2002), "The Rise of the Creative Class), May, retrieved from http://www.washingtonmonthly.com/features/2001/0205.florida.html.

2. Eddie Cuffin (2013), "The 10 Reasons You Should Follow Your Passion and not the Money," August 27, retrieved from http://elitedaily.com/life/motivation/the-10-reasons-you-should-follow-your-passion-and-not-the-money/.

3. Dan Schawbel (2012), "Why Following Your Passion Might not Lead to Career Success," September 17, retrieved from http://www.forbes.com/sites/danschawbel/2012/09/17/why-your-passion-might-not-lead-to-career-success/.

4. Cal Newport (2012), "Why 'Follow Your Passion' is Bad Advice," August 29, retrieved from

http://www.cnn.com/2012/08/29/opinion/passion-career-cal-newport.

5. Marilyn Gregoire (2013), "Why 'Following Your Passion' is Bad Career Advice," July 22, retrieved from http://www.huffingtonpost.com/2013/07/22/sustainable-career_n_3618480.html.

6. Tiffany Marra (n.d.), "The History of 'Authenticity'," retrieved from http://www-personal.umich.edu/~tmarra/authenticity/page2.html.

7. Seth Godin (2009), "Authenticity," February 16, retrieved from http://sethgodin.typepad.com/seths_blog/2009/02/authenticity.html.

8. Dan Schawbel (2013), ""Mark Ecko: How He Built a Billion Dollar Authentic Personal Brand," October 1, retrieved from http://www.forbes.com/sites/danschawbel/2013/10/01/marc-ecko-how-he-built-a-billion-dollar-authentic-personal-brand/.

9. Todd Henry (2013), *Die Empty*, New York: Penguin.

Chapter 6

1. Veronica Maria Jarski (2014), "Top Trends in Content Marketing Hiring," April 8, accessed June 7, 2014 at http://www.marketingprofs.com/chirp/2014/24840/top-trends-in-content-marketing-hiring-infographic.

2. "Local Area Unemployment Statistics" (2014), May 16, accessed June 7, 2014 at http://www.bls.gov/web/laus/laumstrk.htm.

3. Doug Carter (2013), "Demand for Healthcare Professionals High, Growing," January 23, accessed June 7, 2014 at http://www.thestaffingstream.com/2013/01/23/demand-for-healthcare-professionals-remains-high/.

4. Kate Rice (2013), "How Many Travel Agents Are There?" December 2, accessed June 11, 2014 at http://www.travelweekly.com/Travel-News/Travel-Agent-Issues/How-many-travel-agents-are-there-/.

5. Patrick Morris (2013), "7 High-Paying Jobs for the Future of Big Data," November 23, accessed June 13, 2014 at http://www.fool.com/investing/general/2013/11/23/7-high-paying-jobs-for-the-future-of-big-data.aspx.

Chapter 7

1. Brian Tracy (2009), "Success through Goal Setting, Part 1 of 3," January 23, retrieved from http://www.briantracy.com/blog/personal-success/success-through-goal-setting-part-1-of-3/.
2. "Average Annual Hours Actually Worked per Worker" (n.d.), retrieved from http://stats.oecd.org/Index.aspx?DataSetCode=ANHRS.
3. "Chronic Health Conditions Cost U.S. $84 Billion in Lost Productivity, Study Finds" (2013), May 27, retrieved from http://www.huffingtonpost.com/2013/05/07/chronic-health-conditions-lost-productivity-absenteeism-missed-work_n_3232438.html.
4. Gail Sessoms (2014), "Examples of Companies' Wellness Programs," February 19, retrieved from http://www.livestrong.com/article/344920-examples-of-companies-wellness-programs/.
5. Dan Diamond (2013), "Just 8% of People Achieve Their New Year's Resolutions. Here's How They Do It," January 1, retrieved from http://www.forbes.com/sites/dandiamond/2013/01/01/just-8-of-people-achieve-their-new-years-resolutions-heres-how-they-did-it/.
6. "Retail Store Manager Trainee Salaries" (2014), n.d., retrieved from http://www1.salary.com/Retail-Store-Manager-Trainee-salary.html.
7. Brian Tracy (2011), "Building the Courage to Break Out of Your Comfort Zone," November 16, retrieved from http://www.briantracy.com/blog/general/building-the-courage-to-break-out-of-your-comfort-zone/.

Chapter 8

1. Lei Han (2014), "Hard Skills vs. Soft Skills- Difference and Importance," (n.d.), retrieved from https://bemycareercoach.com/soft-skills/hard-skills-soft-skills.html.
2. FINRA Registration and Examination Requirements (n.d.), retrieved from

http://www.finra.org/industry/compliance/registration/qualificatio nsexams/qualifications/p011051.

3. Michelle Jamrisko and Ilan Kolet (2014), "College Tuition Costs Soar: Chart of the Day," August 18, retrieved from http://www.bloomberg.com/news/2014-08-18/college-tuition-costs-soar-chart-of-the-day.html.

4. "The Rising Cost of not Going to College," (2014), February 11, retrieved from http://www.pewsocialtrends.org/2014/02/11/the-rising-cost-of-not-going-to-college/.

5. "HRM0102: Human Resource Management Certificate Program-Online," (n.d.), retrieved from http://www.ocpe.gmu.edu/programs/human_resources/hr_online.php#reqs.

6. Phil Izzo (2014), "Congratulations to Class of 2014, Most Indebted Ever," May 16, retrieved from http://blogs.wsj.com/numbers/congatulations-to-class-of-2014-the-most-indebted-ever-1368/.

7. "Courses" (n.d.), retrieved from https://www.coursera.org/courses.

8. "About Lynda.com," (n.d.), retrieved from http://www.lynda.com/press.

9. Dan Schawbel (2013), *Promote Yourself*, New York: St. Martin's Press.

10. Han (2014)

11. "Overwhelming majority of companies say soft skills are just as important as hard skills, according to a new CareerBuilder survey" (2014), *PR Newswire*, April 10, retrieved from http://search.proquest.com/docview/1514186941?accountid=4886.

12. Bancino, Randy and Zevalkink, Claire (2007), "Soft Skills: The New Curriculum for Hard Core Technical Professionals," *Techniques: Connecting Education & Careers*, 82 (5), 20-22.

13. "Emotional Intelligence and Soft Skills: What Employers Are Seeking" (2012), October 5, retrieved from http://sph.umn.edu/28323/.

14. Rosen, Andrew G. (n.d.), "Soft Skills for Hard Times," retrieved from http://www.jobacle.com/blog/soft-skills-for-hard-times.html.

15. Lei Han (2014), "Soft Skills List- 28 Skills to Working Smart," (n.d.), retrieved from https://bemycareercoach.com/soft-skills/list-soft-skills.html.

16. Cavacini, Michael (2014), "National Survey Reveals 75% of Job Seekers as Unqualified," September 10, retrieved from http://www.businesswire.com/news/home/20140910005092/en/National-Survey-Reveals-75-HR-Professionals-View#.VEGo9vnF_gU.

Chapter 10

1. Darling, D. (2010). *The Networking Survival Guide : Practical Advice to Help You Gain Confidence, Approach People, and Get the Success You Want.* New York: McGraw-Hill Professional.

2. Yeung, R. (2012). *The New Rules of Networking : The Essential Rules and Secrets to Modern Networking.* Singapore: Marshall Cavendish International [Asia] Pte Ltd.

3. Zack, D. (2010). *Networking for People Who Hate Networking : A Field Guide for Introverts, the Overwhelmed, and the Underconnected.* San Francisco: Berrett-Koehler Publishers.

4. Sautter, E., & Crompton, D. (2008). *Seven Days to Online Networking : Make Connections to Advance Your Career and Business Quickly.* Indianapolis, IN: Jist Publishing.

Chapter 13

1. Susan Adams (2014), "Four Ways to Use Facebook to Find a Job," February 6, retrieved from http://www.forbes.com/sites/susanadams/2014/02/06/4-ways-to-use-facebook-to-find-a-job/.

2. Zoe Fox (2011), This is Why You Were Friended or Unfriended (Study), December 19, retrieved from http://mashable.com/2011/12/19/friend-unfriend-facebook/.

3. Willy Franzen (n.d.), Use Facebook Ads to Make Employers Hunt You Down, retrieved from http://www.onedayonejob.com/blog/use-facebook-ads-to-make-employers-hunt-you-down/.

4. Social Networking Fact Sheet (2014), n.d., retrieved from http://www.pewinternet.org/fact-sheets/social-networking-fact-sheet/.

5. Number of Monthly Active Twitter Users Worldwide from 1st Quarter 2010 to 2nd Quarter 2016 (in Millions) (2016), n.d.., retrieved from http://www.statista.com/statistics/282087/number-of-monthly-active-twitter-users/.

6. Press Page (2016), retrieved from http://instagram.com/press/.

7. Jenn Herman (2014), "Instagram Statistics for 2014," February 17, retrieved from http://www.jennstrends.com/instagram-statistics-for-2014/.

8. "Leading Social Networks Worldwide as of December 2014, Ranked by Number of Active Users (in Millions)," (n.d.), retrieved from http://www.statista.com/statistics/272014/global-social-networks-ranked-by-number-of-users/.

9. Brian Honigman (2012), "3 Niche Networks That Will Never be Replaced by Facebook or Twitter,", August 1, retrieved from http://www.businessinsider.com/3-niche-social-networks-that-will-never-be-replaced-by-facebook-or-twitter-2012-8.

10. Venessa Wong (2013), "Hey Job Applicants, Time to Stop the Social Media Sabotage," retrieved from http://www.businessweek.com/articles/2013-06-27/for-job-applicants-social-media-sabotage-is-still-getting-worse.

Chapter 14

1. Craig Smith (2016), "By the Numbers: 133 Amazing LinkedIn Statistics," August 16, retrieved from http://expandedramblings.com/index.php/by-the-numbers-a-few-important-linkedin-stats/.

2. Jeff Bullas (2014), "25 LinkedIn Facts and Statistics You Need to Share," (n.d.), retrieved from http://www.jeffbullas.com/2014/12/02/25-linkedin-facts-and-statistics-you-need-to-share/.

3. Pete Leibman (2014), "Please Change Your LinkedIn Headline Now... Here's Why and How," June 11, retrieved from

https://www.linkedin.com/pulse/20140611214034-7483005-please-change-your-linkedin-headline-now-here-s-why-and-how.

4. Alexis Baird (2014), "Creating a Killer LinkedIn Profile: Tips from Link Humans," July 1, retrieved from http://blog.linkedin.com/2014/07/01/creating-a-killer-linkedin-profile-tips-from-link-humans/.

5. William Arruda (2014), "Three steps to Writing the Perfect LinkedIn Summary," September 7, retrieved from http://www.forbes.com/sites/williamarruda/2014/09/07/three-steps-to-writing-the-perfect-linkedin-summary/.

6. Melissa Llarena (2013), "LinkedIn Challenge Tip 3: How to Fill In the LinkedIn Experience Section," November 1, retrieved from http://melissallarena.com/linkedin/linkedin-challenge-tip-3-fill-linkedin-experience-section%E2%80%8F/.

7. Melonie Dodaro (2013), "21 Steps to the Perfect LinkedIn Profile," February 27, retrieved from http://topdogsocialmedia.com/linkedin-training-creating-the-perfect-profile/.

8. Viveka Von Rosen (2014), "How to Use LinkedIn Publisher to Get More Visibility," July 23, retrieved from at http://www.socialmediaexaminer.com/linkedin-publisher-to-get-visibility/.

9. Miriam Salpeter (n.d.), "LinkedIn's Company Follow Function," retrieved from http://www.job-hunt.org/social-networking/linkedin-company-follow.shtml.

Chapter 15

1. Joe Pulizzi (2012), "Six Useful Content Marketing Definitions," retrieved from http://contentmarketinginstitute.com/2012/06/content-marketing-definition/.

2. Content Marketing Institute (2015), "Original Research," n.d., retrieved from http://contentmarketinginstitute.com/research/.

3. Jill Celeste (2013), "Why You Need Content Marketing for Personal Branding," July 27, retrieved from

http://www.business2community.com/content-marketing/why-you-need-content-marketing-for-personal-branding-0566195.

4. Content Marketing Institute (2015), "Original Research," n.d., retrieved from http://contentmarketinginstitute.com/research/.

5. Lauren I. Labrecque, Ereni Markos, and George R. Milne (2011), "Online Personal Branding: Processes, Challenges, and Implications," *Journal of Interactive Marketing*, 25 (1), 37-50.

6. Susan Adams (2012), "What is a thought leader?" March 16, retrieved from http://www.forbes.com/sites/russprince/2012/03/16/what-is-a-thought-leader/.

7. Mark W. Schaefer and Stanford A. Smith (2013), *Born to Blog*, New York: McGraw-Hill.

8. Invodo (2014), "Video Statistics: The Marketer's Summary 2014," n.d., retrieved from http://www.invodo.com/wp-content/uploads/2014/02/Invodo_Video_Statistics_The_Marketers_Summary_2014.pdf.

9. Cecilia Kang (2014), "Podcasts Are Back – And Making Money," September 25, retrieved from http://www.washingtonpost.com/business/technology/podcasts-are-back--and-making-money/2014/09/25/54abc628-39c9-11e4-9c9f-ebb47272e40e_story.html.

10. Jeff Sanders (2014), "How to Leverage Podcasting to Quickly Grow Your Personal Brand," February 14, retrieved from http://jeffsanders.com/leverage-podcasting/.

11. Patrick Schwerdtfeger (2011), "Leverage Podcasting to Build a Personal Brand," July 1, retrieved from http://www.personalbrandingblog.com/leverage-podcasting-to-build-a-personal-brand/.

12. Kevan Lee (2014), "The Art of Self-Promotion on Social Media," June 19, retrieved from https://blog.bufferapp.com/self-promotion-in-social-media.

13. Demian Farnworth (2015), "Here's How Veteran Search Engine Expert Danny Sullivan Writes," March 11, retrieved from http://www.copyblogger.com/how-danny-sullivan-writes/.

Chapter 16

1. Donna Collins (2011), "The 500-Year Evolution of the Resume, February 12, retrieved from http://www.businessinsider.com/how-resumes-have-evolved-since-their-first-creation-in-1482-2011-2?op=1.

2. Meredith Levinson (2012), "5 Secrets for Beating Applicant Tracking Systems," March 1, retrieved from http://www.cio.com/article/2398753/careers-staffing/5-insider-secrets-for-beating-applicant-tracking-systems.html.

3. Jessica Holbrook Hernandez (2013), "Why Your Resume Should NEVER Have a Resume Statement," January 28, retrieved from http://www.greatresumesfast.com/blog/2013/01/28/why-your-resume-should-never-have-an-objective-statement/.

4. Meredith Levinson (2012), "5 Secrets for Beating Applicant Tracking Systems," March 1, retrieved from http://www.cio.com/article/2398753/careers-staffing/5-insider-secrets-for-beating-applicant-tracking-systems.html.

5. Rachel Rowan Stamper (2015), "5 Marketing Secrets That Will Help Your Resume Get Noticed," n.d., retrieved from https://www.themuse.com/advice/5-marketing-secrets-that-will-help-your-resume-get-noticed.

6. Tracy Lube (2014), "Cover Letter 101: Best Practices to Land an Interview," August 2, retrieved from http://www.slideshare.net/TracyLube/cover-letter-101-best-practices-to-land-an-interview.

7. Pamela Skillings (2014), "Cover Letter Examples that Will Get You Noticed," January 30, retrieved from http://biginterview.com/blog/2014/01/cover-letter-examples.html.

8. Kim Isaacs (n.d.), "10 Cover Letter Don'ts," retrieved from http://career-advice.monster.com/resumes-cover-letters/cover-letter-tips/10-cover-letter-donts/article.aspx.

9. "89% of Employers Open to Viewing Video Resumes, Says Vault" (2007), March 27, retrieved from http://www.businesswire.com/news/home/20070327005962/en/89-Employers-Open-Viewing-Video-Resumes-Vault#.VVHqxI5VgSU.

10. Allison Doyle (n.d.), "Video Resume Tips," retrieved from http://jobsearch.about.com/od/videoresumes/a/videoresume.htm.
11. Rachel Gillett (2014) "How to Create an Infographic Resume that Doesn't Repel Hiring Managers," October 30, retrieved from http://www.fastcompany.com/3037764/hit-the-ground-running/how-to-create-an-infographic-resume-that-doesnt-repel-hiring-managers.

Made in the USA
Middletown, DE
30 October 2016